# TRADITIONAL
# AUSTRALIAN
# VERSE

# TRADITIONAL AUSTRALIAN VERSE

## The Essential Collection

Edited by

# Richard Walsh

ALLEN&UNWIN

First published by Allen & Unwin in 2009

Allen & Unwin
83 Alexander Street
Crows Nest NSW 2065
Australia
Phone:    (61 2) 8425 0100
Fax:       (61 2) 9906 2218
Email:    info@allenandunwin.com
Web:      www.allenandunwin.com

Cataloguing-in-Publication details are available from:
National Library of Australia
www.librariesaustralia.nla.gov

ISBN: 978 1 74237 1 382 (pbk.)

Text designed and typeset in Goudy Old Style 10.5/15 pt by Nada Backovic Designs
Printed and bound in Australia by Griffin Press

10 9 8 7 6 5 4 3 2 1

# Contents

# TO THE END OF THE EARTH IN CHAINS

This is a collection of traditional verse and songs, even doggerel. But it is more than that. It is the story of the first hundred years or so of English-speaking exiles coming to emotional terms with their fate and with the exotic island on which they found themselves marooned. These are white-fellas' songlines, marking the path and its landmarks as a new culture was forged.

As with the poems themselves, which are predominantly ballads, this selection is not merely a whole lot of fine words – there is a narrative here as well. Beginning with the convicts (equal parts nostalgia and defiance), through the optimism of the Roaring Days, to the assured ebullience of *The Bulletin* Bards. There was a rise of patriotism leading up to Federation, but also an awareness that the Australia emerging was somewhat more complex than Paterson's famous 'vision splendid'. As *The Bulletin* Bards grew older, they mourned the loss of their youth and the rise of the great bustling cities and modern technology, which for them meant railways displacing Cobb & Co and steamers displacing the majesty of the old sailing clippers.

At the end of this era, there was the participation by young Australian soldiers in foreign wars. A few, like

'Breaker' Morant, went breezily off to the Boer War; but later came the Great War, when the sense of a Boy's Own Adventure quickly soured and became instead the decimation of a whole generation who had promised so much. And then followed the slow realisation that those boys who had survived the heady madness would be returning to a country that had changed, often beyond recognition.

All these verses have rhythms that lend themselves to the joys of reciting poetry, or singing it. There were other, more ambitious kinds of poetry being written during these years, of course, with their own special rewards. But collected here are the uncomplicated delights of galloping rhyme. It is the language of the street, rather than the elevated and slightly strained language associated with the Heights of Poesy. In making this selection my prejudice has been towards the unpretentious and the unselfconscious.

The order is approximately chronological, but shaped to highlight the different stages in the development of the Australian identity. Thematically the collection ends with the country that will greet C.J. Dennis's immortal Ginger Mick when he returns home, 'When orl the stoushin's over'. Any poems written after 1918 – as, for example, Father Hartigan's charming evocations of rural family life – are only included because in their spirit they illuminate an earlier, less complicated time.

Banjo Paterson and C.J. Dennis in their heyday were recognised internationally as amongst the finest practitioners of light verse in the English language. In our natural desire to be regarded as a country that produces serious artists and writers, we should never feel ashamed that we also produce fine popular entertainers – great black and white artists, pop musicians, stage entertainers, and light versifiers.

This collection was made with no higher purpose than to delight the reader. I hope you get half as much fun out of reading it as I have had from gathering up some of my old-time favourites.

# TRUE PATRIOTS ALL

## *Henry Carter*

From distant climes, o'er wide-spread seas we come,
Though not with much *éclat*, or beat of drum;
True patriots all, for be it understood,
We left our country, for our country's good:
No private views disgrac'd our generous zeal,
What urg'd our travels, was our country's weal;
And none will doubt, but that our emigration
Has proved most useful to the British nation.

---

An anonymous broadside in the possession of the National
Library claims that at the opening of the Sydney Play-house,
16 January 1796, a special prologue was written and recited by
the convicted Irish pickpocket, George Barrington. However,
the eminent scholars Philip Butterss and Elizabeth Webby
assert that the lines were actually written by the English
playwright Henry Carter. Whatever, these are the first eight
lines of that prologue and they are rightly treasured.

*climes* = climate, region
*weal* = well-being

# I, POOR CONVICT

## *Thomas Cavendar*

May the rose of England never blow,
May the Scotch thistle never grow,
May the harp of Ireland never play,
Till I poor convict greets my liberty.

---

The convict Thomas Cavendar tattooed this verse onto his
right arm while he was awaiting transportation in 1830.

# BOTANY BAY

### *Florian Pascal*

Farewell to Old England forever,
Farewell to my old pals as well,
Farewell to the well-known Old Bailee
Where I once used to be such a swell –
Where I once used to be such a swell.

CHORUS:
*Singing too-rall, li-oo-rall, li-ad-di-ty,*
*Singing too-rall, li-oo-rall, li-ay,*
*Singing too-rall, li-oo-rall, li-ad-di-ty*
*Oh, we are bound for Botany Bay –*
*Oh, we are bound for Botany Bay.*

There's the captain as is our commander,
There's the bo'sun and all the ship's crew,
There's the first and the second class passengers,
Knows what we poor convicts goes through –
Knows what we poor convicts goes through.

CHORUS: *Singing too-rall, li-oo-rall, li-ad-di-ty &c.*

'Taint leaving Old England we cares about,
'Taint 'cos we mispells wot we knows,
But becos all we light-finger'd gentry,

Hops around with a log on our toes —
Hops around with a log on our toes.

CHORUS: *Singing too-rall, li-oo-rall, li-ad-di-ty &c.*

Oh, had I the wings of a turtle-dove,
I'd soar on my pinions so high,
Slap bang to the arms of my Polly love,
And in her sweet presence I'd die —
And in her sweet presence I'd die.

CHORUS: *Singing too-rall, li-oo-rall, li-ad-di-ty &c.*

Now all my young Dookies and Duchesses,
Take warning from what I've to say,
Mind all is your own as you touch-es-es,
Or you'll meet us in Botany Bay —
Or you'll meet us in Botany Bay.

CHORUS: *Singing too-rall, li-oo-rall, li-ad-di-ty &c.*

---

This ballad, which is exceedingly popular among modern
Australians, was not composed by a convict, nor indeed
by an Australian, but by the Englishman Florian Pascal
(a.k.a. Joseph Williams) for the comedy *Little Jack Shepherd*,
which played in London in 1885 and in Melbourne in 1886.

# LAMENT
## (UPON VAN DIEMEN'S SHORE)

### *Sarah Collins*

They chain us two by two, and whip and lash along,
They cut off our provisions, if we do the least thing wrong,
They march us in the burning sun, until our feet are sore,
So hard's our lot now we are got upon Van Diemen's shore.

We labour hard from morn to night, until our bones do ache,
Then every one, they must obey, their mouldy beds must make;
We often wish, when we lay down, we ne'er may rise no more,
To meet our savage governors upon Van Diemen's shore.

Every night when I lay down, I wash my straw with tears,
While wind upon that horrid shore to whistle in our ears;
Those dreadful beasts upon that land around our cots do roar;
Most dismal is our doom upon Van Diemen's shore.

Come all young men and maidens, do bad company forsake,
If tongue can tell our overthrow, it would make your heart to ache;
You girls, I pray, be ruled by me, your wicked ways give o'er,
For fear, like us, you spend your days upon Van Diemen's shore.

---

This short lament was unearthed by the poet John Kinsella. Apparently
little is known of 'Miss Sarah Collins', but her verse was composed in 1839.

# PORT PHILLIP! LAND OF MANY WONDERS

*Anonymous*

Port Phillip! Land of many wonders;
Land of lightning; land of thunders;
Land of various reptiles evil;
Land of heat would scorch the devil;
Land of every savage vice;
Land of Christian avarice;
Land of emus, kangaroos;
Land of parrots, cockatoos;
Land of pelicans, black swans;
Land of possums and tuans;
Land of bandicoots, wild cats;
Land of Platipusses, rabbit rats,
Land of march flies and mosquitos;
Land of pumpkins and tomatoes;
Land whose various winged tribes
Are yet unsung by learned scribes;
Land of gloomy desolation;
Land of reckless dissipation;
Land of damper, tea, and mutton,
Enough to satiate a glutton;
On damper, mutton, and bohea,
Poor bushmen fare three times a day.

Land of murderers, burglars, robbers;
Pickpockets, lawyers, and landjobbers.
From every turn my fate directs,
I feel the gloomiest effects –
By day by hosts of flies invaded,
At night by wild dogs serenaded.

---

This lugubrious paean was first published on 22 January 1844 in the *Geelong Advertiser*, where it was described by its anonymous author as 'Scraps from a Bushman's Note Book'.

*tuan* = Aboriginal name for the flying glider
*rabbit rat* = the jumping mouse or hapalote
*bohea* = low-grade tea
*landjobbers* = land sharks, who make excessive profits from land speculation

# ODOROUS MELBOURNE

### J. Brenchley

Odorous Melbourne, city of stinks!
What fragrance o'erhovers thy cesspools and sinks;
I have smelt many smells, but the richest *per se*,
May justly be claim'd, luscious Melbourne, by thee.
When the sun has gone down, and the wind's in the west,
And the night-air is heavy, by closeness opprest,
From thy fam'd open drains, a soft essence is thrown,
An odour delightful, uniquely thine own.
  Odorous Melbourne – delectable Melbourne!
  Odoriferous Melbourne – sweet Stinkomalee!

Cologne may boast proudly – that sanctified town –
Of the forty odd stinks that enhance its renown;
But thine has a raciness rivall'd by none,
Like all the full forty commingled in one.
And though time-honour'd odours pervade the Fleet Ditch,
With its full-flavour'd mud and perfumeries rich,
Let them boast as they may: to this creed I incline,
It is not a patch on these brave drains of thine.
  Odorous Melbourne – delectable Melbourne!
  Odoriferous Melbourne – soft Stinkomalee!

. . . *over*

This extraordinary outburst was included in the author's *May Bloom and Wattle Blossoms*, which was 'published for the author by George Robertson, Melbourne, in 1876'.

*o'erhovers* = floats above
*Fleet Ditch* = the infamous sewer outlet for London, where all of the gutters of the city washed into the river, made memorable by Alexander Pope in his *The Dunciad*: 'To where Fleet-ditch with disemboguing streams Rolls the large tribute of dead dogs to Thames'

# BOUND FOR SOUTH AUSTRALIA

**Anonymous**

In South Australia I was born
Heave away! Haul away!
South Australia round Cape Horn
And we're bound for South Australia.

CHORUS:
*Haul away, you rolling king*
*Heave away! Haul away!*
*All the way you'll hear me sing*
*And we're bound for South Australia.*

As I walked out one morning fair
Heave away! Haul away!
It's there I met Miss Nancy Blair
And we're bound for South Australia.

CHORUS: *Haul away, you rolling king &c.*

There ain't but one thing grieves my mind
Heave away! Haul away!
It's to leave Miss Nancy Blair behind
And we're bound for South Australia.

CHORUS: *Haul away, you rolling king &c.*

I run her all night, I run her all day
Heave away! Haul away!
Run her before we sailed away
And we're bound for South Australia.

CHORUS: *Haul away, you rolling king &c.*

I shook her up, I shook her down
Heave away! Haul away!
I shook her round and round and round
And we're bound for South Australia.

CHORUS: *Haul away, you rolling king &c.*

And as you wollop round Cape Horn
Heave away! Haul away!
You'll wish that you had never been born
And we're bound for South Australia.

CHORUS: *Haul away, you rolling king &c.*

---

This sea shanty was originally sung on the British docks
as the large wool clippers left on their runs to Australia. A
version of it was collected by Laura Smith from sailors in
Tyneside and printed in her *The Music of the Waters* in 1888.
It continues to be a popular folk song, frequently recorded.

# ODE TO WESTRALIA

## The Boulder Bard

Land of Forrests, fleas and flies,
Blighted hopes and blighted eyes,
Art thou hell in earth's disguise,
  Westralia?

Art thou some volcanic blast
By volcanoes spurned, outcast?
Art unfinished – made the last
  Westralia?

Wert thou once the chosen land
Where Adam broke God's one command?
That He in wrath changed thee to sand,
  Westralia!

Land of politicians silly,
Home of wind and willy-willy,
Land of blanket, tent and billy,
  Westralia.

Home of brokers, bummers, clerks,
Nest of sharpers, mining sharks,

Dried up lakes and desert parks,
  Westralia!

Land of humpies, brothels, inns,
Old bag huts and empty tins,
Land of blackest, grievous sins
  Westralia.

---

This was first published anonymously on 9 April 1899 in the *Kalgoorlie Sun*. It was the source of considerably controversy at that time. 'Boulder Bard' also published that year as 'Willy-Willy'; while his identity is unproven, it is supposed to have been a certain William Williams, who resided at Hopkins Street, Boulder.

*Forrests* = a reference to the intrepid brothers and explorers, Alexander and John Forrest. The mining entrepreneur 'Twiggy' Forrest is their descendant.

# THE OLD BUSH SONGS

In 1906 Banjo Paterson, by then established as the great balladist of *The Bulletin*, published with Angus & Robertson *The Old Bush Songs*, a collection of traditional ballads 'Composed and sung in the Bushranging, Digging, and Overlanding Days'. As Paterson explained in his preface:

*The object of the present publication is to gather together all the old bush songs that are worth remembering. Apart from other considerations, there are many Australians who will be reminded by these songs of the life of the shearing sheds, the roar of the diggings townships, and the campfires of the overlanders. The diggings are all deep·sinking now, the shearing is done by contract, and the cattle are sent by rail to market, while newspapers travel all over Australia; so there will be no more bush ballads composed and sung, as these were composed and sung, as records of the early days of the nation. In their very roughness, in their absolute lack of any mention of home ties or of the domestic affections, they proclaim their genuineness. They were collected from all parts of Australia, and have been patched together by the compiler to the best of his ability, with the idea of presenting the song as nearly as possible as it was sung, rather than attempting to soften any roughness or irregularity of metre.*

Paterson also noted: 'Attempts to ascertain the names of the authors have produced contradictory statements, and no doubt some of the songs were begun by one man and finished or improved by another, or several others.'

In 1957 the poets Douglas Stewart and Nancy Keesing produced a greatly expanded version of Paterson's original collection and so revived its popularity. The first seven songs in this section are from Paterson's *The Old Bush Songs* and then there are two from the 1957 update.

It is amazing that there were some very good ballads uncollected by these esteemed anthologists, such evergreens as *Click Go the Shears* and *Banks of the Condamine*, which I have also included. My selection is rounded out by a couple of racier songs, which were probably not to the taste of these pioneering, and somewhat stitched-up, predecessors, and also one of the earliest songs indisputably written by a woman, Mary Hannah Foott's 'Where the Pelican Builds Her Nest'.

# ON THE ROAD TO GUNDAGAI

*Anonymous*

Oh, we started down from Roto when the sheds had all cut out.
We'd whips and whips of Rhino as we meant to push about,
So we humped our blues serenely and made for Sydney town,
With a three-spot cheque between us, as wanted knocking down.

CHORUS:
  *But we camped at Lazy Harry's, on the road to Gundagai*
  *The road to Gundagai! Not five miles from Gundagai!*
  *Yes, we camped at Lazy Harry's, on the road to Gundagai.*

Well, we struck the Murrumbidgee near the Yanko in a week,
And passed through old Narrandera and crossed the Burnet Creek.
And we never stopped at Wagga, for we'd Sydney in our eye.
But we camped at Lazy Harry's, on the road to Gundagai.

CHORUS: *But we camped, &c.*

Oh, I've seen a lot of girls, my boys, and drunk a lot of beer,
And I've met with some of both, chaps, as has left me mighty queer;
But for beer to knock you sideways, and for girls to make you sigh,
You must camp at Lazy Harry's, on the road to Gundagai.

CHORUS: *You must camp, &c.*

Well, we chucked our blooming swags off, and we walked into the bar,
And we called for rum-an'-raspb'ry and a shilling each cigar.
But the girl that served the pizen, she winked at Bill and I
And we camped at Lazy Harry's, not five miles from Gundagai.

CHORUS: *And we camped, &c.*

In a week the spree was over and the cheque was all knocked down,
So we shouldered our "Matildas", and we turned our backs on town,
And the girls they stood a nobbler as we sadly said "Good bye",
And we tramped from Lazy Harry's, not five miles from Gundagai.

CHORUS: *And we tramped, &c.*

---

*Roto* = small township north of Hillston in south-west
New South Wales
*whips of Rhino* = rhino-hide whips, which were traditionally
used by South African herdsmen
*spot* = £100
*humped our blues* and *shouldered our Matildas* = to carry one's
swag; the name 'bluey' came from the blue blankets they carried
*Yanko* = Yanco Creek, one of the main tributaries of
the Murrumbidgee; the town of Yanco, near Leeton in
New South Wales, was renamed Yanko in 1892 and
then officially reverted to Yanco (a Wiradjuri word
meaning 'the sound of running water') in 1928
*Burnet Creek* = Burnett Creek, a minor waterway
in the Yanco area
*pizen* = alternative name for the famous Bohemian brewing town
of Plzen (in German, *Pilsen*) and here simply meaning a pilsener
*nobbler* = a measure of spirits

# BOLD JACK DONAHOO

### Anonymous

In Dublin town I was brought up, in that city of great fame
My decent friends and parents, they will tell to you the same.
It was for the sake of five hundred pounds I was sent across the main,
For seven long years, in New South Wales, to wear a convict's chain.

CHORUS:
*Then come, my hearties, we'll roam the mountains high!*
*Together we will plunder, together we will die!*
*We'll wander over mountains and we'll gallop over plains,*
*For we scorn to live in slavery, bound down in iron chains.*

I'd scarce been there twelve months or more upon the Australian shore,
When I took to the highway, as I'd oft-times done before.
There was me and Jacky Underwood, and Webber and Webster, too.
These were the true associates of bold Jack Donahoo.

CHORUS: *Then come, &c.*

Now, Donahoo was taken, all for a notorious crime,
And sentenced to be hanged upon the gallows-tree so high.
But when they came to Sydney gaol, he left them in a stew,
And when they came to call the roll, they missed bold Donahoo.

CHORUS: *Then come, &c.*

As Donahoo made his escape, to the bush he went straight-way.
The people they were all afraid to travel night or day,
For every week in the newspapers there was published some-thing new
Concerning this dauntless hero, the bold Jack Donahoo!

CHORUS: *Then come, &c.*

As Donahoo was cruising, one summer's afternoon,
Little was his notion his death was near so soon,
When a sergeant of the horse police discharged his car-a-bine,
And called aloud on Donahoo to fight or to resign.

CHORUS: *Then come, &c.*

"Resign to you – you cowardly dogs! A thing I ne'er will do,
For I'll fight this night with all my might," cried bold Jack Donahoo.
"I'd rather roam these hills and dales, like wolf or kangaroo,
Than work one hour for Government!" cried bold Jack Donahoo.

CHORUS: *Then come, &c.*

He fought six rounds with the horse police until the fatal ball,
Which pierced his heart and made him start, caused Donahoo to fall.
And as he closed his mournful eyes, he bade this world Adieu,
Saying, "Convicts all, both large and small, say prayers for Donahoo!"

CHORUS: *Then come, &c.*

There are many ballads celebrating Bold Jack Donahoo/ Donahoe/Donahue, but this is the version in *The Old Bush Songs*. John Donohoe (the *Australian Dictionary of Biography*'s preferred spelling) arrived at Sydney Cove on 2 January 1825, having been sentenced to transportation for life on a charge of 'intent to commit felony'. He and two companions were sentenced to death in 1828 for robbery, but Donohoe escaped. On 1 September 1830, he was shot dead by Trooper Muggleston at Bringelly Scrub near Campbelltown in western Sydney.

*the main* = a poetic term for the open sea
*car-a-bine* = 'carabine', the earliest (French) spelling of carbine

# THE WILD COLONIAL BOY

### *Anonymous*

'Tis of a wild Colonial boy, Jack Doolan was his name,
Of poor but honest parents he was born in Castlemaine.
He was his father's only hope, his mother's only joy,
And dearly did his parents love the wild Colonial boy.

CHORUS:
    Come, all my hearties, we'll roam the mountains high,
    Together we will plunder, together we will die.
    We'll wander over valleys, and gallop over plains,
    And we'll scorn to live in slavery, bound down with iron chains.


He was scarcely sixteen years of age when he left his father's home,
And through Australia's sunny clime a bushranger did roam.
He robbed those wealthy squatters, their stock he did destroy,
And a terror to Australia was the wild Colonial boy.

    *CHORUS: Come, all my hearties, &c.*


In sixty-one this daring youth commenced his wild career,
With a heart that knew no danger, no foeman did he fear.
He stuck up the Beechworth mail coach, and robbed Judge MacEvoy,
Who trembled, and gave up his gold to the wild Colonial boy.

*CHORUS: Come, all my hearties, &c.*

He bade the Judge "Good morning", and told him to beware,
That he'd never rob a hearty chap that acted on the square,
And never to rob a mother of her son and only joy,
Or else you may turn outlaw, like the wild Colonial boy.

*CHORUS: Come, all my hearties, &c.*

One day as he was riding the mountain side along,
A-listening to the little birds, their pleasant laughing song,
Three mounted troopers rode along – Kelly, Davis, and FitzRoy.
They thought that they would capture him – the wild Colonial boy.

*CHORUS: Come, all my hearties, &c.*

"Surrender now, Jack Doolan, you see there's three to one.
Surrender now, Jack Doolan, you daring highwayman."
He drew a pistol from his belt, and shook the little toy.
"I'll fight, but not surrender," said the wild Colonial boy.

*CHORUS: Come, all my hearties, &c.*

He fired at Trooper Kelly, and brought him to the ground,
And in return from Davis received a mortal wound.
All shattered through the jaws he lay still firing at FitzRoy,
And that's the way they captured him – the wild Colonial boy.

*CHORUS: Come, all my hearties, &c.*

. . . *over*

This famous song was first published in 1881, and for the next hundred years controversy raged over whether Jack Doolan was real or mythical. The most persuasive account of his life is contained in Allen Mawer's *The Life and Legend of Jack Doolan, the Wild Colonial Boy* (Mulini Press 2004).

# THE OLD BARK HUT

### Anonymous

Oh, my name is Bob the Swagman, before you all I stand,
And I've had many ups and downs while travelling through the land.
I once was well-to-do, my boys, but now I am stumped up,
And I'm forced to go on rations in an old bark hut.

CHORUS:
*In an old bark hut. In an old bark hut.*
*I'm forced to go on rations in an old bark hut.*

Ten pounds of flour, ten pounds of beef, some sugar and some tea,
That's all they give to a hungry man, until the Seventh Day.
If you don't be moighty sparing, you'll go with a hungry gut,
For that's one of the great misfortunes in an old bark hut.

CHORUS:
*In an old bark hut. In an old bark hut.*
*For that's one of the great misfortunes in an old bark hut.*

The bucket you boil your beef in has to carry water, too,
And they'll say you're getting mighty flash if you should ask for two.
I've a billy, and a pint pot, and a broken-handled cup,
And they all adorn the table in the old bark hut.

CHORUS:
*In an old bark hut. In an old bark hut.*
*And they all adorn the table in the old bark hut.*

Faith, the table is not made of wood, as many you have seen,
For if I had one half so good, I'd think myself serene,
'Tis only an old sheet of bark; God knows when it was cut,
It was blown from off the rafters of the old bark hut.

CHORUS:
*In an old bark hut. In an old bark hut.*
*It was blown from off the rafters of the old bark hut.*

And of furniture, there's no such thing, 'twas never in the place,
Except the stool I sit upon – and that's an old gin-case.
It does us for a safe as well, but you must keep it shut,
Or the flies would make it canter round the old bark hut.

CHORUS:
*In an old bark hut. In an old bark hut.*
*Or the flies would make it canter round the old bark hut.*

If you should leave it open, and the flies should find your meat,
They'll scarcely leave a single piece that's fit for man to eat.
But you mustn't curse, nor grumble – what won't fatten will fill up.
For what's out of sight is out of mind in an old bark hut.

CHORUS:
*In an old bark hut. In an old bark hut.*
*For what's out of sight is out of mind in an old bark hut.*

In the summer time, when the weather's warm, this hut is nice and cool,
And you'll find the gentle breezes blowing in through every hole.
You can leave the old door open, or you can leave it shut,
There's no fear of suffocation in the old bark hut.

CHORUS:
*In an old bark hut. In an old bark hut.*
*There's no fear of suffocation in the old bark hut.*

In the winter time – preserve us all – to live in there's a treat
Especially when it's raining hard, and blowing wind and sleet.
The rain comes down the chimney, and your meat is black with soot –
That's a substitute for pepper in an old bark hut.

CHORUS:
*In an old bark hut. In an old bark hut.*
*That's a substitute for pepper in an old bark hut.*

I've seen the rain come in this hut just like a perfect flood,
Especially through that great big hole where once the table stood.
There's not a blessed spot, me boys, where you could lay your nut,
But the rain is sure to find you in the old bark hut.

CHORUS:
*In an old bark hut. In an old bark hut.*
*But the rain is sure to find you in the old bark hut.*

So beside the fire I make me bed, and there I lay me down,
And think myself as happy as the king that wears a crown.

But as you'd be dozing off to sleep a flea will wake you up,
Which makes you curse the vermin in the old bark hut.

CHORUS:
*In an old bark hut. In an old bark hut.*
*Which makes you curse the vermin in the old bark hut .*

Faith, such flocks of fleas you never saw, they are so plump and fat,
And if you make a grab at one, he'll spit just like a cat.
Last night they got my pack of cards, and were fighting for the cut,
I thought the devil had me in the old bark hut.

CHORUS:
*In an old bark hut. In an old bark hut.*
*I thought the devil had me in the old bark hut.*

So now, my friends, I've sung my song, and that as well as I could,
And I hope the ladies present won't think my language rude,
And all ye younger people, in the days when you grow up,
Remember Bob the Swagman, and the old bark hut.

CHORUS:
*In an old bark hut. In an old bark hut.*
*Remember Bob the Swagman, and the old bark hut.*

# THE EUMERELLA SHORE

## Anonymous

There's a happy little valley on the Eumerella shore,
Where I've lingered many happy hours away,
On my little free selection I have acres by the score,
Where I unyoke the bullocks from the dray.

CHORUS:
*To my bullocks then I say*
*No matter where you stray,*
*You will never be impounded any more;*
*For you're running, running, running on the duffer's piece of land,*
*Free selected on the Eumerella shore.*

When the moon has climbed the mountains and the stars are shining bright,
Then we saddle up our horses and away,
And we yard the squatters' cattle in the darkness of the night,
And we have the calves all branded by the day.

CHORUS:
*Oh, my pretty little calf,*
*At the squatter you may laugh,*
*For he'll never be your owner any more;*
*For you're running, running, running on the duffer's piece of land,*
*Free selected on the Eumerella shore.*

If we find a mob of horses when the paddock rails are down,
Although before they're never known to stray,
Oh, quickly will we drive them to some distant inland town,
And sell them into slav'ry far away.

CHORUS:
*To Jack Robertson we'll say*
*You've been leading us astray,*
*And we'll never go a-farming any more;*
*For it's easier duffing cattle on the little piece of land*
*Free selected on the Eumerella shore.*

---

John ('Jack') Robertson was five times Premier of New South Wales and a lifelong advocate of 'free selection', the establishment of small farms excised from squatters' vast holdings. But these were often uneconomic and the farmers lived in hardship. This is a hymn to the illegal alternative – *duffing* (rustling livestock).

There are many variants of the place name in the title. The problem is that what is today called the Eumeralla River is in western Victoria, whereas the reference to Robertson would place the disillusioned cocky in New South Wales. One of the most common variant titles is *The Numerella Shore* and the Umerella (Numerella) River flows near Cooma.

# THE DYING STOCKMAN

## *Horace Flower*

A strapping young stockman lay dying,
His saddle supporting his head;
His two mates around him were crying,
As he rose on his pillow and said:

*CHORUS:*
*"Wrap me up with my stockwhip and blanket,*
*And bury me deep down below,*
*Where the dingoes and crows can't molest me,*
*In the shade where the coolibahs grow.*

"Oh! had I the flight of the bronzewing,
Far o'er the plains would I fly,
Straight to the land of my childhood,
And there would I lay down and die.

*CHORUS: Wrap me up, &c.*

"Then cut down a couple of saplings,
Place one at my head and my toe,
Carve on them cross, stockwhip, and saddle,
To show there's a stockman below.

*CHORUS: Wrap me up, &c.*

"Hark! there's the wail of a dingo,
Watchful and weird, I must go,
For it tolls the death-knell of the stockman
From the gloom of the scrub down below.

CHORUS: *Wrap me up, &c.*

"There's tea in the battered old billy;
Place the pannikins out in a row,
And we'll drink to the next merry meeting,
In the place where all good fellows go.

CHORUS: *Wrap me up, &c.*

"And oft in the shades of the twilight,
When the soft winds are whispering low,
And the dark'ning shadows are falling,
Sometimes think of the stockman below."

CHORUS: *Wrap me up, &c.*

---

Paterson appears to have been unaware of the authorship of this ballad when he included it in *Old Bush Songs*. It was written by Horace Flower and first published in a western Victorian newspaper, the *Portland Mirror*, on 8 July 1885.

# BRINGING HOME THE COWS

### Anonymous

Shadows of the twilight falling
　On the mountain's brow,
To each other birds are calling,
　In the leafy bough.
Where the daisies are a-springing,
And the cattle bells are ringing,
Comes my Mary, gaily singing,
　Bringing home the cows.

By a bush the pathway skirted,
　Room for two allows.
All the cornfields are deserted,
　Idle are the ploughs.
Striving for wealth's spoil and booty,
Farmer boys have finished duty,
When I meet my little beauty,
　Bringing home the cows.

Tender words and kind addresses,
　Most polite of bows,
Rosy cheeks and wavy tresses
　Do my passions rouse
Dress so natty and so cleanly,
Air so modest and so queenly.
Oh! so haughty, yet serenely,
　Bringing home the cows.

Arm-in-arm together walking,
  While the cattle browse,
Earnestly together talking,
  Plighting lovers' vows.
Where the daisies are a-springing,
Wedding bells will soon be ringing,
Then we'll watch our servant bringing
  Mine and Mary's cows.

# WALLABY STEW

### *Anonymous*

Poor Dad he got five years or more as everybody knows,
And now he lives in Maitland Jail with broad arrows on his clothes,
He branded all of Brown's clean-skins and never left a tail,
So I'll relate the family's woes since Dad got put in jail.

CHORUS:
*So stir the wallaby stew,*
*Make soup of the kangaroo tail,*
*I tell you things is pretty tough*
*Since Dad got put in jail.*

Our sheep were dead a month ago, not rot but blooming fluke,
Our cow was boozed last Christmas Day by my big brother Luke,
And Mother has a shearer cove for ever within hail,
The family will have grown a bit since Dad got put in jail.

Our Bess got shook upon a bloke, he's gone we don't know where,
He used to act around the shed, but he ain't acted square;
I've sold the buggy on my own, the place is up for sale,
That won't be all that isn't junked when Dad comes out of jail.

They let Dad out before his time, to give us a surprise.
He came and slowly looked around, and gently blessed our eyes,

He shook hands with the shearer cove and said he thought things stale,
So he left him here to shepherd us and battled back to jail.

---

Stewart and Keesing noted that a poem titled 'When Dad
Comes Out of Gaol' was published in *The Bulletin* in 1897
under the authorship of Cecil Poole. It is very similar, but
they judge it to be derivative; they believe 'Wallaby Stew'
was composed much earlier by author or authors unknown.

*clean-skins* = unbranded animals
*never left a tail* = Dad's kindness knew no limits – he did
not merely take custody of Brown's new-born lambs,
he also docked their tails
*fluke* = an infestation of the liver

# SPRINGTIME BRINGS ON THE SHEARING

### Anonymous

Oh the springtime it brings on the shearing
And it's then you will see them in droves
To the west country stations all steering
A-seeking a job off the coves

CHORUS:
*With a ragged old swag on my shoulder*
*And a billy quart-pot in my hand*
*I tell you we'll astonish the new chums*
*To see how we travel the land*

You may talk of your mighty exploring
Of Landsborough McKinley and King
But I feel I should only be boring
On such frivolous subjects to sing

For discovering mountains and rivers
There's one for a gallon I'd back
Who'd beat all your Stuart's to shivers
It's the men on the Wallaby Track

From Billabone Murray and Loddon
To the far Tartiara and back

The hills and the plains are well trodden
By the men on the Wallaby Track

And after the shearing is over
And the wool season's all at an end
It is then that you will see those flash shearers
Making johnny cakes round in the bend

---

This was included in the 1957 Stewart and Keesing *Old Bush Songs* collection. It had been originally derived from E.J. Overbury's 1865 poem 'The Wallaby Track', and subsequently worked over by a variety of camp-fire singers.

John King was the sole survivor of the disastrous Burke and Wills expedition. William Landsborough and John McKinlay (the preferred spelling) were two of the explorers who searched for them in 1861. But the most accomplished explorer of the inland had been John McDougall Stuart.

The Loddon River meets the Murray near Swan Hill and presumably the Billabone is a long-lost place name from those parts. Tatiara, as it is called today, is over the border in South Australia.

*coves* = originally meant the station owners or managers
*new chums* = recent arrivals
*johnny cakes* = the small dampers eaten by shearers when their money had run out

# CLICK GO THE SHEARS

**Anonymous**

Out on the board the old shearer stands,
Grasping his shears in his long bony hands,
Fixed is his gaze on a bare-bellied joe.
Glory – if he gets her, won't he make the ringer go!

*CHORUS:*
*Click go the shears, boys! Click, click, click!*
*Wide is his blow and his hands move quick,*
*The ringer looks around and is beaten by a blow,*
*And curses the old snagger with the blue-bellied joe.*

In the middle of the floor in his cane-bottomed chair
Is the boss of the board, with eyes everywhere,
Notes well each fleece as it comes to the screen,
Paying strict attention if it's taken off clean.

CHORUS: *Click go the shears, boys! Click, click, click!* &c.

The colonial-experience man he is there, of course,
With his shiny leggin's, just got off his horse,
Casting round his eye like a real connoisseur
Whistling the old tune *I'm the Perfect Lure.*

CHORUS: *Click go the shears, boys! Click, click, click!* &c.

The tar-boy is there a-waiting in demand,
With his blackened tar-pot and his tarry hand.
Sees one old sheep with a cut upon its back;
Here's what he's waiting for – "Tar here, Jack!"

CHORUS: *Click go the shears, boys! Click, click, click! &c.*

Shearing is all over and we've all got our cheques;
Roll up your swag for we're off on the tracks.
The first pub we come to it's there we'll have a spree
And everyone that comes along it's "Come and drink with me!"

CHORUS: *Click go the shears, boys! Click, click, click! &c.*

Down by the bar the old shearer stands,
Grasping his glass in his thin bony hands;
Fixed is his gaze on a green-painted keg
Glory – he'll get down on it ere he stirs a peg!

CHORUS: *Click go the shears, boys! Click, click, click! &c.*

There we leave him standing, shouting for all hands,
Whilst all around him every shouter stands.
His eyes are on the cask, which is now lowering fast.
He works hard, he drinks hard and goes to hell at last.

CHORUS: *Click go the shears, boys! Click, click, click! &c.*

You take off the belly-wool, clean out the crutch;
Go up the neck, for the rules they are such;

You clean round the horns first, shoulder go down,
One blow up the back and you then turn around.

CHORUS: *Click go the shears, boys! Click, click, click! &c.*

Click! Click! That's how the shears go.
Click! Click! So awfully quick.
You pull out a sheep – he'll give a kick.
And still hear your shears going – click, click, click!

CHORUS: *Click go the shears, boys! Click, click, click, &c.*

One of the gold diggers' favourites was a song by the popular American composer Henry C. Work, which began: 'High in the belfry the old sexton stands / Grasping the rope with his thin bony hands'. An anonymous shearer borrowed Work's tune, and some ideas from his words, and created 'Click Go the Shears'. Although it was very popular for decades in many versions, and remains so, it was only first published in 1946.

*board* = the floor of a shearing shed
*bare-bellied* (also '*blue-bellied*') *joe* = ewes with little wool on their belly; 'joe' (or 'yeo') is an English dialect word for ewe
*ringer* = fastest shearer in the shed
*snagger* = an unskilful shearer who leaves 'snags' of wool on the sheep
*as it comes to the screen* = as it comes to the table, at which the fleeces are classed into different grades
*colonial-experience man* = an English gentleman, sampling

life in 'the colonies' by working on a station
*tar-boy* = the lad who applied tar to any snicks the shearers made
*he'll get down on it ere he stirs a peg* = he'll get stuck into it before
he stirs a leg
*shouting for all hands* = buying drinks for everyone in the bar

# BANKS OF THE CONDAMINE

### Anonymous

Hark, hark, the dogs are barking – I can no longer stay
The boys have all gone shearing, I heard the publican say.
And I must be off in the morning, love, before the sun do shine,
To meet the Roma shearers on the banks of the Condamine.

*Oh, Willie, dearest Willie, don't leave me here to mourn;*
*Don't make me curse and rue the day that ever I was born.*
*For parting with you, Willie, is like parting with my life;*
*So stay and be a selector, love, and I will be your wife.*

Oh, Nancy, dearest Nancy, you know that I must go –
The squatters are expecting me their shearing for to do.
And when I'm on the board, my love, I'll think of you with pride
And my shears they will go freely when I'm on the whipping side.

*Oh, I'll cut off my yellow hair and go along with you.*
*I'll dress myself in men's attire and be a shearer too.*
*I'll cook and count your tally, love, whilst ringer-o you shine*
*And I'll wash your greasy moleskins on the banks of the Condamine.*

Oh, Nancy, dearest Nancy, you know you cannot go –
The boss has given his orders no woman may do so.
And your delicate constitution isn't equal unto mine,
To eat the ram-stag mutton on the banks of the Condamine.

But when the shearing's over, I'll make of you my wife,
I'll get a boundary-riding job and settle down for life.
And when the day's work's done, my love, and the evening it is fine
I'll tell of them sandy cobblers on the banks of the Condamine.

The Condamine is one of the legendary Queensland tributaries
of the Darling River. In Victoria and southern New South
Wales, this charming duet was known as 'The Banks of
the Riverine' and was first published under that title in
1894. It had been derived from 'The Banks of the Nile', a
British ballad dating from the beginning of the nineteenth
century, where the singer was heading off to the Napoleonic
Wars. In the Australian variant, he is sometimes going off
to a horse-breaking camp rather than a shearing shed.

*selector* = a struggling small land-holder
*ram-stag* = a ram no longer required for servicing the flock,
so it is castrated and fattened for slaughter. Such mutton
was apparently not for discerning palates.
*boundary riding* = the job of checking out a station's
boundary fences
*sandy cobblers* = folklorist Edgar Waters ingeniously explains
this thus: 'Cobbler is an old-fashioned word for shoemaker;
the sheep which the shearer left in his pen until the end of
a work period were likely to be hard to shear (because, for
example, there was a lot of sand in their wool); such sheep
were kept till the last and so – in the stereotyped shearers'
joke – compared with the cobbler, who stuck to his last.'

# THE SHEARER'S DREAM

### *Anonymous*

O I dreamt I shore in a shearing shed and it was a dream of joy,
For every one of the rouseabouts was a girl dressed up as a boy.
Dressed up like a page in a pantomime, the prettiest ever seen –
They had flaxen hair, they had coal-black hair, and every shade between.

CHORUS:
*There was short plump girls, there was tall slim girls, and the handsomest ever seen;*
*They was four foot five, they was six foot high, and every shade between.*

The shed was cooled by electric fans that was over every shute;
The pens was of polished mahogany and everything else to suit;
The huts had springs to the mattresses and the tucker was simply grand,
And every night by the billabong we danced to a German band.

CHORUS: *There was short plump girls, there was tall slim girls, &c.*

Our pay was the wool on the jumbucks' backs, so we shore till all was blue;
The sheep was washed afore they was shore, and the rams were scented too;
And we all of us cried when the shed cut out, in spite of the long hot days,
For every hour them girls waltzed in with whisky and beer on trays.

CHORUS: *There was short plump girls, there was tall slim girls, &c.*

There was three of them girls to every chap, and as jealous as they could be;
There was three of them girls to every chap, and six of them picked on me;

We was drafting them out for the homeward track, and sharing them round like steam ..
When I woke with my head in the blazing sun – to find it a shearer's dream!

CHORUS: *There was short plump girls, there was tall slim girls, &c.*

---

First published in *Children of the Bush* in 1902, this is
usually attributed to Henry Lawson. In fact, he probably
re-worked an earlier version of unknown origin.

*shore till all was blue* = shorn until the bluish skin of the sheep could
be seen through the thin covering of wool left after close shearing
*when the shed cut out* = when the shearing in that shed had finished
*drafting out* = a countryman's term for selecting
the best (usually of animals)

# BLUEY BRINK

*Anonymous*

There once was a shearer by name Bluey Brink,
A devil for work and a terror for drink;
He could shear a full hundred each day without fear
And drink without winking four gallons of beer.

Now Jimmy the barman, who served out the drink,
He hated the sight of this here Bluey Brink,
Who stayed much too late and who came much too soon –
At morning, at evening, at night and at noon.

One day as Jimmy was cleaning the bar
With sulphuric acid he kept in a jar,
Along comes this shearer a-bawling with thirst
Saying "Whatever you've got, Jim, just give me the first."

Now it ain't in the history, you won't find it in print,
But that shearer drunk acid with never a wink,
Saying "That's the stuff, Jimmy! Why, strike me stone dead,
This'll make me the ringer of Stephenson's shed!"

All through that long day, as he served up the beer,
Poor Jimmy was sick with his trouble and fear.
Too anxious to argue, too worried to fight,
He saw that poor shearer a corpse in his fright.

But early next morning, when he opened the door,
Well there was that shearer a-yelling for more –
With his eyebrows all singed and his whiskers deranged,
And holes in his hide like a dog with the mange.

Says Jimmy, "And how did you find the new stuff?"
Says Bluey, "It's fine, but I've not had enough.
It gives me great courage to shear and to fight,
But why does that stuff set me whiskers alight?

"I thought I knew grog, but I must have been wrong –
The stuff that you gave me was proper and strong.
It set me to coughing, and you know I'm no liar,
But every damn cough set me whiskers on fire."

The exact provenance of this song is unknown, but it may
have been composed in the twentieth century. The fanciful
comments of folklorist A.L. Lloyd are worth quoting: 'Old Dad
Adams of Cowra, New South Wales, used to sing this song.
Rumour had it the pubs didn't stock anything strong enough
for Old Dad. It was said he would bore a hole in the bottom of
a silo and suck out the fermented juice of the ensilage through
a straw. To one expressing disbelief, the answer was: "All right,
look for yourself. All the silos around Cowra hav' got little
holes bored in 'em." Anyway, Old Dad didn't make the song.
Perhaps it was made by the Speewa sleeper-cutter, who went
into a chemist's and called for prussic acid with a vitriol chaser,
adding: "And don't go dilutin' it with that ammonia, neither."'

# LAMBING DOWN

### *Anonymous*

I'm a broken-hearted shearer, I'm ashamed to show my face,
The way that I got lambed down is a sin and a disgrace;
I put a cheque together, and thought that it would do,
So I just slipped into Orange for to spend a week or two.

I thought I was no flat, so resolved to cut it fat;
I dressed myself up in my best, put a poultice round my hat;
I went to have a nobbler at a certain house in town,
Where the barmaid she was cautioned for to lamb a fellow down.

I would get up in the morning to have a glass of stout;
She cost me many a shilling, for she was in every shout,
She would toss me up at Yankee Grab, and keep me on the booze;
But somehow or the other I was always bound to lose.

My money getting short, I resolved to know my fate;
I asked this pretty barmaid if she would be my mate,
When she said, 'Young man, on my feelings don't encroach,
I'm a decent married woman, and my husband drives the coach.'

I had two-and-six in silver and half-a-bar of soap,
A box of Cockle's pills and a pot of Holloway's;
I thought to turn a farmer and grow pumpkins near the town,
But she squashed all my pumpkins when she had me lambed down.

I had two old shirts, but they were all in rags;
A pair of moleskin trousers and a hat without a crown.
This was my ten years' gathering when clearing out of town;
But it's nothing when you're used to it to do a lambing down.

---

*lambed down* = spent money lavishly in the pub, usually encouraged by mine host
*flat* = a new-chum, who was gullible to the local sharps
*poultice* = sometimes a solid wad of money, which he may have carried inside the lining of his hat
*cautioned* = instructed
*Yankee Grab* = a dice game
*Cockle's pills and a pot of Holloway's* = Cockle's Anti-Bilious Pills and Thomas Holloway's 'Cure-all' Ointment Pot were popular panaceas of the nineteenth century

# NINE MILES FROM GUNDAGAI

*Anonymous*

I'm used to drivin' bullock teams
Across the hills and plains;
I've teamed outback these forty years
In blazin' droughts and rains.
I've lived a heap of troubles through,
Without a bloomin' lie;
But I can't forget what happened me
Nine miles from Gundagai.

'Twas gettin' dark, the team got bogged,
The axle snapped in two;
I lost me matches and me pipe,
Now what was I to do?
The rains come down, 'twas bitter cold,
And hungry too was I;
And the dog shat in the tucker-box
Nine miles from Gundagai.

Some blokes I know has all the luck,
No matter how they fall;
But there was I, Lord love a duck,
No flamin' luck at all.
I couldn't make a pot of tea
Nor keep me trousers dry;

And the dog shat in the tucker-box,
Nine miles from Gundagai.

I could forgive the blinkin' tea ,
I could forgive the rain;
I could forgive the dark and cold,
And go through it again.
I could forgive me rotten luck;
But hang me till I die,
 I won't forgive that bloody dog,
Nine miles from Gundagai.

---

The origins of this ballad are amongst the most hotly
contested in Australian folklore; however, its earliest version
is a poem called 'Bullocky Bill', published by 'Bowyang
Yorke' in the *Gundagai Times* in 1857. It told of a hardy,
stoic and unlucky teamster who got bogged at Five Mile
Creek, a popular meeting place five miles from Gundagai.

In 1967 John Meredith, of The Bushwhackers band, wrote
an article called 'Along the Road to Gundagai – but how
many miles'. He said: 'Over thirty of our old bush songs and
ballads are about Gundagai – the struggles of her people and
the troubles and fun that the bullockies and the shearers had
there in the second half of the last century.' In the 1880s 'Nine
Miles from Gundagai' had emerged – the distance mysteriously
changing and the dog now 'sitting' on the tuckerbox. But,
as Meredith dryly observed, the song could hardly have
lived so long if the dog had merely *sat* on the tuckerbox.

Salesman and balladeer Jack Moses in the 1920s created a cleaned-up version of 'Nine Miles from Gundagai', in which the dog sits on, and guards, the tuckerbox. This proved immensely popular and subsequently the famous Dog On The Tuckerbox monument was constructed outside Gundagai, and unveiled before a large and appreciative crowd by the Australian Prime Minister, Joe Lyons, in 1932. As it happened, the organising committee placed the monument five miles from the town, not for sound historical reasons but because that seemed better for tourism.

Confusingly, the popular musician Jack O'Hagan published his version in 1937. It was called 'Where the Dog Sits on the Tuckerbox (5 miles from Gundagai)'.

# WHERE THE PELICAN BUILDS HER NEST

## Mary Hannay Foott

The horses were ready, the rails were down,
But the riders lingered still;
One had a parting word to say,
And one had his pipe to fill.
Then they mounted, one with a granted prayer,
And one with a grief unguessed.
"We are going," they said, as they rode away
"Where the Pelican builds her nest!"

They had told us of pastures wide and green,
To be sought past the sunset's glow;
Of rifts in the ranges by opal lit;
And gold 'neath the river's flow.
And thirst and hunger were banished words
When they spoke of that unknown West;
No drought they dreaded, no flood they feared,
Where the pelican builds her nest!

The creek at the ford was but fetlock deep
When we watched them crossing there;
The rains have replenished it thrice since then,
And thrice has the rock lain bare.

But the waters of Hope have flowed and fled,
And never from blue hill's breast
Come back – by the sun and the sands devoured
Where the pelican builds her nest!

Mary Hannay Foott (1846–1918) married and then settled
first at Bourke in New South Wales and later in south-western
Queensland. In 1885, the year after her husband died, she
started a school and published this much-anthologised ballad.

The unexplored parts of Australia are sometimes spoken of
by the bushmen of western Queensland as the home of the
pelican, a bird whose nesting place is seldom located.

# THE PIONEER POETS
## Adam Lindsay Gordon and Henry Kendall

The bush songs had been mainly anonymous and were often inspired by existing ballads brought to Australia by its earliest convicts and settlers. Such verse was intended to be sung or recited; it existed in many impromptu variations. These were the crude inventions of men with limited education.

First Adam Lindsay Gordon and then Henry Kendall brought to this tradition a poetic sensibility. Their creations were printed and intended to be read; the best of them were later collected and published in book form. Gordon's most famous collection, *Bush Ballads and Galloping Rhymes*, was published in 1870; Kendall is best remembered for *Leaves from Australian Forests*, published in 1869.

Adam Lindsay Gordon (1833–70) was from an English military family, who despatched him to Adelaide when he was twenty. He tried his hand at both politics and business, without success. He moved to Victoria and ultimately became a professional rider with some small fame at the track, particularly as a steeplechaser. His poetry was published in newspapers of the day but, after a number of severe falls and some financial embarrassment, he sunk into low spirits.

The day after *Galloping Rhymes* appeared in book form, he bumped into Henry Kendall, who showed him a favourable review he had written for publication. Nonetheless, overwhelmed by his indebtedness, the next day Gordon walked into the bush and shot himself.

Henry Kendall (1839–82) was Australian-born; his grandfather was a minister of religion and his father a missionary. He tried his hand at journalism and his friends found a number of sinecures for him; although his poetry was regularly published in newspapers of the day, he spent much of his life in penury and indeed confessed to the poet George Gordon McCrae that he could not attend A.L. Gordon's funeral because he was penniless.

Kendall ultimately descended into alcoholism and melancholia. He escaped a charge of forgery on the grounds of temporary insanity and spent time in the Gladesville Hospital for the Insane. He ultimately died from a chill and consumption.

Gordon and Kendall produced verse that was more self-consciously poetic than the traditional ballads they had inherited; they wrote as educated men. They offered a greater variety of subject matter – for example, the ocean, the rainforest and horse riding for pleasure. Their mood was subtler: the bravado of 'The Dying Stockman' becomes more complexly nostalgic in Gordon's 'The Sick Stockrider'. They experimented with new rhyme patterns and in their rhythms they freed themselves from the relentless iambs (dum-DUM) of the old bush songs.

These two poets are clearly forerunners of *The Bulletin* Bards, and particularly Paterson and Lawson, and nowhere more so than in 'How We Beat The Favourite', where the subject matter points forward to 'The Man From Snowy River' and the internal rhymes and the distinctive trochees (DUM-dum) of the alternating lines anticipate the bewitching cleverness of the opening stanzas of 'Clancy of the Overflow'. For the reader, it is like changing gears.

# HOW WE BEAT THE FAVOURITE

### Adam Lindsay Gordon

'Aye squire,' said Stevens, 'they back him at evens;
The race is all over, bar shouting, they say;
The Clown ought to beat her, Dick Neville is sweeter
Than ever – he swears he can win all the way.

'A gentleman rider – well, I'm an outsider,
But if he's a gent who the mischief's a jock?
You swells mostly blunder, Dick rides for the plunder,
He rides, too, like thunder – he sits like a rock.

'He calls "hunted fairly" a horse that has barely
Been stripp'd for a trot within sight of the hounds,
A horse that at Warwick beat Birdlime and Yorick,
And gave Abdelkader at Aintree nine pounds.

'They say we have no test to warrant a protest;
Dick rides for the lord and stands in with a steward;
The light of their faces they show him – his case is
Prejudged and his verdict already secured.

'But none can outlast her, and few travel faster,
She strides in her work clean away from The Drag;
You hold her and sit her, she couldn't be fitter,
Whenever you hit her she'll spring like a stag.

'And p'rhaps the green jacket, at odds though they back it,
May fall, or there's no knowing what may turn up.
The mare is quite ready, sit still and ride steady,
Keep cool; and I think you may just win the Cup.'

Dark-brown with tan muzzle, just stripped for the tussle,
Stood Iseult, arching her neck to the curb,
A lean head and fiery, strong quarters and wiry,
A loin rather light, but a shoulder superb.

Some parting injunction, bestowed with great unction,
I tried to recall, but forgot like a dunce,
When Reginald Murray, full tilt on White Surrey,
Came down in a hurry to start us at once.

'Keep back in the yellow! Come up on Othello!
Hold hard on the chestnut! Turn around on The Drag!
Keep back there on Spartan! Back you, sir, in tartan!
So, steady there, easy!' and down went the flag.

We started, and Kerr made strong running on Mermaid,
Through furrows that led to the first stake-and-bound,
The crack, half extended, look'd bloodlike and splendid,
Held wide on the right where the headland was sound.

I pulled hard to baffle her rush with the snaffle,
Before her two-thirds of the field got away;
All through the wet pasture where floods of the last year
Still loitered, they clotted my crimson with clay.

The fourth fence, a wattle, floor'd Monk and Bluebottle;
The Drag came to grief at the blackthorn and ditch,
The rails toppled over Redoubt and Red Rover,
The lane stopped Lycurgus and Leicestershire Witch.

She passed like an arrow Kildare and Cock Sparrow,
And Mantrap and Mermaid refused the stone wall;
And Giles on The Greyling came down at the paling,
And I was left sailing in front of them all.

I took them a burster, nor eased her nor nursed her
Until the Black Bullfinch led into the plough,
And through the strong bramble we bored with a scramble –
My cap was knock'd off by the hazel-tree bough.

Where furrows looked lighter I drew the rein tighter –
Her dark chest all dappled with flakes of white foam,
Her flanks mud-bespattered, a weak rail she shattered –
We landed on the turf with our heads turn'd for home.

Then crash'd a low binder, and then close behind her
The sward to the strokes of the favourite shook;
His rush roused her mettle, yet ever so little
She shorten'd her stride as we raced at the brook.

She rose when I hit her. I saw the stream glitter,
A wide scarlet nostril flared close to my knee,
Between sky and water The Clown came and caught her,
The space that he cleared was a caution to see.

And forcing the running, discarding all cunning,
A length to the front went the rider in green;
A long strip of stubble, and then the big double,
Two stiff flights of rails with a quickset between.

She raced at the rasper, I felt my knees grasp her,
I found my hands give to her strain on the bit;
She rose when The Clown did – our silks as we bounded
Brush'd lightly, our stirrups clash'd loud as we lit.

A rise steeply sloping, a fence with stone coping –
The last – we diverged round the base of the hill
His path was the nearer, his leap was the clearer,
I flogg'd up the straight and he led sitting still.

She came to his quarter, and on still I brought her,
And up to his girth, to his breastplate she drew,
A short prayer from Neville just reach'd me, 'The Devil!'
He mutter'd – lock'd level the hurdles we flew.

A hum of hoarse cheering, a dense crowd careering,
All sights seen obscurely, all shouts vaguely heard;
'The green wins!' 'The crimson!' The multitude swims on,
And figures are blended and features are blurr'd.

'The horse is her master!' 'The green forges past her!'
'The Clown will outlast her!' 'The Clown wins!' 'The Clown!'
The white railing races with all the white faces,
The chestnut outpaces, outstretches the brown.

On still past the gateway she strains in the straightway,
Still struggles, 'The Clown by a short neck at most,'
He swerves, the green scourges, the stand rocks and surges,
And flashes and verges, and flits the white post.

Aye! so ends the tussle – I knew the tan muzzle
Was first, though the ring-men were yelling 'Dead heat!'
A nose I could swear by, but Clarke said, 'The mare by
A short head.' And that's how the favourite was beat.

Sub-titled 'A Lay of the Loamshire Hunt Cup', this is apparently
Gordon's recounting of a Warwickshire race he witnessed as
a youth, before his despatch to Australia. It remains the most
popular of his poems. Although it contains a fair amount of
steeplechasing jargon, the bare bones of this dramatic story
are clear: the narrator, a gentleman-rider in crimson, is on
the mare Iseult ('dark-brown with tan muzzle') and she is up
against the much-fancied favourite, The Clown, a stallion
ridden by Dick Neville in his distinctive green jacket.

# THE SICK STOCKRIDER

## *Adam Lindsay Gordon*

Hold hard Ned! Lift me down once more, and lay me in the shade.
Old man, you've had your work cut out to guide
Both horses, and to hold me in the saddle when I sway'd,
All through the hot, slow, sleepy, silent ride.

The dawn at "Moorabinda" was a mist rack dull and dense,
The sunrise was a sullen, sluggish lamp;
I was dozing in the gateway at Arbuthnot's bound'ry fence,
I was dreaming on the Limestone cattle camp.

We crossed the creek at Carricksford, and sharply through the haze,
And suddenly the sun shot flaming forth;
To southward lay "Katawa" with the sandpeaks all ablaze,
And the flush'd field of Glen Lomond lay to the north.

Now westward winds the bridle that leads to Lindisfarm,
And yonder looms the double-headed Bluff;
From the far side of the first hill, when the skies are clear and calm,
You can see Sylvester's woolshed fair enough.

Five miles we used to call it from our homestead to the place
Where the big tree spans the roadway like an arch;
'Twas here we ran the dingo down that gave us such a chase
Eight years ago – or was it nine? – last March.

'Twas merry in the glowing morn, among the gleaming grass,
To wander as we've wandered many a mile,
And blow the cool tobacco cloud and watch the white wreaths pass,
Sitting loosely in the saddle all the while.

'Twas merry 'mid the blackwoods, when we spied the station roofs,
To wheel the wild scrub cattle at the yard,
With a running fire of stockwhips and a fiery run of hoofs;
Oh! the hardest day was never then too hard!

Aye! we had a glorious gallop after "Starlight" and his gang,
When they bolted from Sylvester's on the flat;
How the sun-dried reed-beds crackled, how the flint-strewn ranges rang
To the strokes of "Mountaineer" and "Acrobat".

Hard behind them in the timber, harder still across the heath,
Close behind them through the tea-tree scrub we dash'd;
And the golden-tinted fern leaves, how they rustled underneath!
And the honeysuckle osiers, how they crash'd!

We led the hunt throughout, Ned, on the chestnut and the grey,
And the troopers were three hundred yards behind,
While we emptied our six-shooters on the bushrangers at bay,
In the creek with stunted box-tree for a blind!

There you grappled with the leader, man to man and horse to horse,
And you roll'd together when the chestnut rear'd
He blazed away and missed you in that shallow watercourse –
A narrow shave – his powder singed your beard!

In these hours when life is ebbing, how those days when life was young
Come back to us; how clearly I recall
Even the yarns Jack Hall invented, and the songs Jem Roper sung;
And where are now Jem Roper and Jack Hall?

Aye! nearly all our comrades of the old colonial school,
Our ancient boon companions, Ned, are gone;
Hard livers for the most part, somewhat reckless as a rule,
It seems that you and I are left alone.

There was Hughes, who got in trouble through that business with the cards,
It matters little what became of him;
But a steer ripp'd up MacPherson in the Cooraminta yards,
And Sullivan was drown'd at Sink-or-swim.

And Mostyn – poor Frank Mostyn – died at last a fearful wreck,
In "the horrors", at the Upper Wandingong;
And Carisbrooke, the rider, at the Horsefall broke his neck,
Faith! the wonder was he saved his neck so long!

Ah! those days and nights we squandered at the Logans' in the glen –
The Logans, man and wife, have long been dead.
Elsie's tallest girl seems taller than your little Elsie then;
And Ethel is a woman grown and wed.

I've had my share of pastime, and I've done my share of toil,
And life is short – the longest life a span;
I care not now to tarry for the corn or for the oil,
Or for the wine that maketh glad the heart of man.

For good undone and gifts misspent and resolutions vain,
'Tis somewhat late to trouble. This I know –
I should live the same life over, if I had to live again;
And the chances are I go where most men go.

The deep blue skies wax dusky, and the tall green trees grow dim,
The sward beneath me seems to heave and fall;
And sickly, smoky shadows through the sleepy sunlight swim,
And on the very sun's face weave their pall.

Let me slumber in the hollow where the wattle blossoms wave,
With never stone or rail to fence my bed;
Should the sturdy station children pull the bush flowers on my grave,
I may chance to hear them romping overhead.

# THE SWIMMER

### Adam Lindsay Gordon

With short, sharp, violent lights made vivid,
　To southward far as the sight can roam,
Only the swirl of the surges livid,
　The seas that climb and the surfs that comb.

Only the crag and the cliff to nor'ward,
　And the rocks receding, and reefs flung forward,
Waifs wreck'd seaward and wasted shoreward,
　On shallows sheeted with flaming foam.

A grim, grey coast and a seaboard ghastly,
　And shores trod seldom by feet of men –
Where the batter'd hull and the broken mast lie,
　They have lain embedded these long years ten.

Love! Love! When we wander'd here together,
Hand in hand! Hand in hand through the sparkling weather,
From the heights and hollows of fern and heather,
　God surely loved us a little then.

The skies were fairer and shores were firmer –
　The blue sea over the bright sand roll'd;
Babble and prattle, and ripple and murmur,
　Sheen of silver and glamour of gold.

So girt with tempest and wing'd with thunder,
   And clad with lightning and shod with sleet,
The strong winds treading the swift waves under
   The flying rollers with frothy feet.

One gleam like a bloodshot sword-blade swims on
The sky-line, staining the green gulf crimson,
A death stroke fiercely dealt by a dim sun,
   That strikes through his stormy winding-sheet.

O, brave white horses! You gather and gallop,
   The storm sprite loosens the gusty reins;
Now the stoutest ship were the frailest shallop
   In your hollow backs, on your high arch'd manes.

I would ride as never a man has ridden
In your sleepy, swirling surges hidden,
To gulfs foreshadow'd thro' strifes forbidden,
   Where no light wearies and no love wanes.

---

This highly impressionistic poem is one of the most dramatic in
Australian literature. With its inventive rhymes, its insistent
consonants and frequent alliteration, it is well suited to recitation.
Sir Edward Elgar ultimately set it to music as the fifth and last
composition in his song-cycle, *Sea Pictures*, and it is that version,
an abridgement of the original, that is reproduced here. Sung by
Dame Janet Baker and others, Elgar's setting of 'The Swimmer' has
established itself as a classic in the international vocal repertoire.

# LIFE IS MOSTLY FROTH AND BUBBLE

### Adam Lindsay Gordon

Hark! The bells of distant cattle
Waft across the range,
Through the golden-tufted wattle,
Music low and strange;
Like the marriage of peal fairies
Comes the tinkling sound,
Or like chimes of sweet St Mary's
On far English ground.

How my courser champs the snaffle,
And with nostrils spread,
Snorts and scarcely seems to ruffle
Fern leaves with his tread;
Cool and pleasant on his haunches
Blows the evening breeze,
Through the overhanging branches
Of the wattle trees.

Onward! to the Southern Ocean
Glides the breath of Spring.
Onward, with a dreamy motion,
I, too, glide and sing –

Forward! forward! still we wander –
Tinted hills that lie
In the red horizon yonder –
Is the goal so nigh?

Whisper, spring-wind, softly singing,
Whisper in my ear;
Respite and nepenthe bringing,
Can the goal be near?
Laden with the dew of vespers,
From the fragrant sky,
In my ear the wind that whispers
Seems to make reply –

"Question not, but live and labour
'Til yon goal be won,
Helping every feeble neighbour,
Seeking help from none;
Life is mostly froth and bubble,
Two things stand like stone,
Kindness in another's trouble,
*Courage* in your own."

---

This is an excerpt from the final section of Gordon's much
longer poem, 'Ye Wearie Wayfarer'. The opening lines here
will have reminded contemporary readers of Gray's popular
'Elegy Written in a Country Church-yard'. Gordon's poem

too is a classic elegy, and the last stanza in this excerpt
is justly famous and much-quoted. It is inscribed on the
poet's gravestone in Brighton Cemetery, Melbourne.

*my courser champs the snaffle* = my swift horse bites into his bridle

# BELL-BIRDS

*Henry Kendall*

By the channels of coolness the echoes are calling,
And down the dim gorges I hear the creek falling;
It lives in the mountain where moss and the sedges
Touch with their beauty the banks and the ledges.
Through breaks of the cedar and sycamore bowers
Struggles the light that is love to the flowers;
And, softer than slumber, and sweeter than singing,
The notes of the bell-birds are running and ringing.

The silver-voiced bell-birds, the darlings of day-time,
They sing in September their songs of the May-time;
When shadows wax strong, and thunder-bolts hurtle,
They hide with their fear in the leaves of the myrtle;
When rain and the sunbeams shine mingled together,
They start up like fairies that follow fair weather;
And straightway the hues of their feathers unfolden,
Are the green and the purple, the blue and the golden.

October, the maiden of bright yellow tresses,
Loiters for love in the cool wildernesses;
Loiters, knee-deep, in the grasses to listen.
Where dripping rocks gleam and the leafy pools glisten:
Then is the time when the water-moons splendid
Break with their gold, and are scattered or blended

Over the creeks, till the woodlands have warning
Of songs of the bell-bird and wings of the morning.

Welcome as waters unkissed by the summers
Are the voices of bell-birds to thirsty far-corners,
When fiery December sets foot in the forest,
And the need of the wayfarer presses the sorest,
Pent in the ridges for ever and ever,
The bell-birds direct him to spring and to river,
With ring and with ripple, like runnels whose torrents
Are toned by the pebbles and leaves in the currents.

Often I sit, looking back to a childhood
Mixt with the sights and the sounds of the wildwood,
Longing for power and the sweetness to fashion.
Lyrics with beats like the heart-beats of passion;
Songs interwoven of lights and of laughters
Borrowed from bell-birds in far forest rafters;
So I might keep in the city and alleys
The beauty and strength of the deep mountain valleys,
Charming to slumber the pain of my losses
With glimpses of creeks and a vision of mosses.

---

A bellbird (its usual spelling today) is the popular name for the
bell-miner, a honey-eater found in the remaining rainforests of
south-eastern Australia. Kendall's poem is a song of praise for
the bird itself and for the subtle pleasures of Springtime (the
Antipodean 'May-time') in the mountain valleys of northern
New South Wales, where he spent some of his formative years.

# THE LAST OF HIS TRIBE

## Henry Kendall

He crouches, and buries his face on his knees,
And hides in the dark of his hair;
For he cannot look up to the storm-smitten trees,
Or think of the loneliness there –
Of the loss and the loneliness there.

The wallaroos grope through the tufts of the grass,
And turn to their coverts for fear;
But he sits in the ashes and lets them pass
Where the boomerangs sleep with the spear –
With the nullah, the sling and the spear.

Uloola, behold him! The thunder that breaks
On the tops of the rocks with the rain,
And the wind which drives up with the salt of the lakes,
Have made him a hunter again –
A hunter and fisher again.

For his eyes have been full with a smouldering thought;
But he dreams of the hunts of yore,
And of foes that he sought, and of fights that he fought
With those who will battle no more –
Who will go to the battle no more.

It is well that the water which tumbles and fills,
Goes moaning and moaning along;
For an echo rolls out from the sides of the hills,
And he starts at a wonderful song –
At the sound of a wonderful song.

And he sees, through the rents of the scattering fogs,
The corroboree warlike and grim,
And the lubra who sat by the fire on the logs,
To watch, like a mourner, for him –
Like a mother and mourner for him.

Will he go in his sleep from these desolate lands,
Like a chief, to the rest of his race,
With the honey-voiced woman who beckons and stands,
And gleams like a dream in his face –
Like a marvellous dream in his face?

# A.B. ('BANJO') PATERSON
## (1864–1941)

Andrew Barton Paterson was the direct heir of the old bush songs tradition, which he greatly cherished, but he took its galloping rhymes and droll humour to dizzying new heights. In 1885 he began submitting poems to *The Bulletin* under the pseudonym 'The Banjo' and was immediately published there, beginning in the February.

By 1895 his ballads had become so popular that Angus & Robertson published a collection of the best of them under the title *The Man from Snowy River and Other Verses*. Its first edition sold out within a week and it went through four editions in six months, making Paterson second only to Kipling in popularity among living poets then writing in English. The London *Times*, in its review of his book, compared him favourably with the Empire's favourite poet, who in fact wrote a congratulatory letter to A&R.

Paterson, the son of a grazier, was born near Orange and then moved when he was seven to a property at Illalong, near Yass in southern New South Wales. He was schooled in Sydney and became first a solicitor and later a journalist of distinction. He was an accomplished sportsman and a notable horseman. He rode to hounds with the Sydney

Hunt Club, became one of the colony's best polo players and, as an amateur rider, competed at Randwick and Rosehill.

The Banjo lived a long, productive and prosperous life. His poetry comprised three major collections; he wrote two novels, many shorter prose pieces and a book for children. However, he is today mainly remembered for the best of his ballads in *The Man from Snowy River and Other Verses*. Yet notable among his later output is the iconic 'Waltzing Matilda', which was written in 1895 under circumstances that still remain contentious.

# THE MAN FROM SNOWY RIVER

### A.B. *Paterson*

There was movement at the station, for the word had passed around
 That the colt from old Regret had got away,
And had joined the wild bush horses – he was worth a thousand pound,
 So all the cracks had gathered to the fray.
All the tried and noted riders from the stations near and far
 Had mustered at the homestead overnight,
For the bushmen love hard riding where the wild bush horses are,
 And the stock-horse snuffs the battle with delight.

There was Harrison, who made his pile when Pardon won the cup,
 The old man with his hair as white as snow;
But few could ride beside him when his blood was fairly up –
 He would go wherever horse and man could go.
And Clancy of the Overflow came down to lend a hand,
 No better horseman ever held the reins;
For never horse could throw him while the saddle-girths would stand,
 He learnt to ride while droving on the plains.

And one was there, a stripling on a small and weedy beast,
 He was something like a racehorse undersized,
With a touch of Timor pony – three parts thoroughbred at least –
 And such as are by mountain horsemen prized.
He was hard and tough and wiry – just the sort that won't say die –
 There was courage in his quick impatient tread;

And he bore the badge of gameness in his bright and fiery eye,
  And the proud and lofty carriage of his head.

But still so slight and weedy, one would doubt his power to stay,
  And the old man said, 'That horse will never do
For a long and tiring gallop – lad, you'd better stop away,
  Those hills are far too rough for such as you.'
So he waited sad and wistful – only Clancy stood his friend –
  'I think we ought to let him come,' he said;
'I warrant he'll be with us when he's wanted at the end,
  For both his horse and he are mountain bred.

'He hails from Snowy River, up by Kosciusko's side,
  Where the hills are twice as steep and twice as rough,
Where a horse's hoofs strike firelight from the flint stones every stride,
  The man that holds his own is good enough.
And the Snowy River riders on the mountains make their home,
  Where the river runs those giant hills between;
I have seen full many horsemen since I first commenced to roam,
  But nowhere yet such horsemen have I seen.'

So he went – they found the horses by the big mimosa clump –
  They raced away towards the mountain's brow,
And the old man gave his orders, 'Boys, go at them from the jump,
  No use to try for fancy riding now.
And, Clancy, you must wheel them, try and wheel them to the right.
  Ride boldly, lad, and never fear the spills,
For never yet was rider that could keep the mob in sight,
  If once they gain the shelter of those hills.'

So Clancy rode to wheel them – he was racing on the wing
  Where the best and boldest riders take their place,
And he raced his stock-horse past them, and he made the ranges ring
  With the stockwhip, as he met them face to face.
Then they halted for a moment, while he swung the dreaded lash,
  But they saw their well-loved mountain full in view,
And they charged beneath the stockwhip with a sharp and sudden dash,
  And off into the mountain scrub they flew.

Then fast the horsemen followed, where the gorges deep and black
  Resounded to the thunder of their tread,
And the stockwhips woke the echoes, and they fiercely answered back
  From cliffs and crags that beetled overhead.
And upward, ever upward, the wild horses held their way,
  Where mountain ash and kurrajong grew wide;
And the old man muttered fiercely, 'We may bid the mob good day,
  No man can hold them down the other side.'

When they reached the mountain's summit, even Clancy took a pull,
  It well might make the boldest hold their breath,
The wild hop scrub grew thickly, and the hidden ground was full
  Of wombat holes, and any slip was death.
But the man from Snowy River let the pony have his head,
  And he swung his stockwhip round and gave a cheer,
And he raced him down the mountain like a torrent down its bed,
  While the others stood and watched in very fear.

He sent the flint stones flying, but the pony kept his feet,
  He cleared the fallen timber in his stride,

And the man from Snowy River never shifted in his seat –
 It was grand to see that mountain horseman ride.
Through the stringy barks and saplings, on the rough and broken ground,
 Down the hillside at a racing pace he went;
And he never drew the bridle till he landed safe and sound,
 At the bottom of that terrible descent.

He was right among the horses as they climbed the further hill,
 And the watchers on the mountain standing mute,
Saw him ply the stockwhip fiercely, he was right among them still,
 As he raced across the clearing in pursuit.
Then they lost him for a moment, where two mountain gullies met
 In the ranges, but a final glimpse reveals
On a dim and distant hillside the wild horses racing yet,
 With the man from Snowy River at their heels.

And he ran them single-handed till their sides were white with foam.
 He followed like a bloodhound on their track,
Till they halted cowed and beaten, then he turned their heads for home,
 And alone and unassisted brought them back.
But his hardy mountain pony he could scarcely raise a trot,
 He was blood from hip to shoulder from the spur;
But his pluck was still undaunted, and his courage fiery hot,
 For never yet was mountain horse a cur.

And down by Kosciusko, where the pine-clad ridges raise
 Their torn and rugged battlements on high,
Where the air is clear as crystal, and the white stars fairly blaze
 At midnight in the cold and frosty sky,

And where around the Overflow the reedbeds sweep and sway
 To the breezes, and the rolling plains are wide,
The man from Snowy River is a household word to-day,
 And the stockmen tell the story of his ride.

'The Man From Snowy River' vies with 'Waltzing Matilda'
and Dorothea Mackellar's 'My Country' as Australia's favourite
poem. It was first published in *The Bulletin* in April 1890 and is
set where the Burrinjuck Dam is located today. Here The Banjo
helped round up brumbies as a child and later owned property.
Jack Riley is the horseman most often claimed as the original
Man from Snowy River, but there are other claimants and there
were many other fearless riders in the district at that time.

The poem inspired a silent film in 1920 and a very popular film
in 1982, starring Tom Burlinson and Sigrid Thornton (Kirk
Douglas, somewhat incongruously, played Harrison). This in
turn inspired a sequel and a successful TV series of the same
name. The poem also inspired a famous sequence in the opening
ceremony of the Sydney Olympic Games in 2000, and in 2002
that presentation was developed as an arena spectacular version.

On this basis it can be fairly stated that no Australian poem
comes near it for its impact on the national imagination.

# CLANCY OF THE OVERFLOW

### A.B. *Paterson*

I had written him a letter which I had, for want of better
  Knowledge, sent to where I met him down the Lachlan, years ago,
He was shearing when I knew him, so I sent the letter to him,
  Just 'on spec', addressed as follows, 'Clancy, of The Overflow'.

And an answer came directed in a writing unexpected,
  (And I think the same was written with a thumb-nail dipped in tar)
'Twas his shearing mate who wrote it, and verbatim I will quote it:
  'Clancy's gone to Queensland droving, and we don't know where he are.'

\* \* \*

In my wild erratic fancy visions come to me of Clancy
  Gone a-droving 'down the Cooper' where the Western drovers go;
As the stock are slowly stringing, Clancy rides behind them singing,
  For the drover's life has pleasures that the townsfolk never know.

And the bush hath friends to meet him, and their kindly voices greet him
  In the murmur of the breezes and the river on its bars,
And he sees the vision splendid of the sunlit plains extended,
  And at night the wond'rous glory of the everlasting stars.

\* \* \*

I am sitting in my dingy little office, where a stingy
  Ray of sunlight struggles feebly down between the houses tall,

And the foetid air and gritty of the dusty, dirty city
 Through the open window floating, spreads its foulness over all.

And in place of lowing cattle, I can hear the fiendish rattle
 Of the tramways and the 'buses making hurry down the street,
And the language uninviting of the gutter children fighting,
 Comes fitfully and faintly through the ceaseless tramp of feet.

And the hurrying people daunt me, and their pallid faces haunt me
 As they shoulder one another in their rush and nervous haste,
With their eager eyes and greedy, and their stunted forms and weedy,
 For townsfolk have no time to grow, they have no time to waste.

And I somehow rather fancy that I'd like to change with Clancy,
 Like to take a turn at droving where the seasons come and go,
While he faced the round eternal of the cash-book and the journal –
 But I doubt he'd suit the office, Clancy, of 'The Overflow'.

---

First published in *The Bulletin* on 21 December 1889, this poem
is based on the correspondence between Paterson, who worked
as a city solicitor, and a man called Thomas Gerald Clancy.
Clancy makes a brief appearance in 'The Man from Snowy River',
published the following year. 'Clancy of the Overflow' was set
to music by the notable Australian composer, Albert Arlen, and
has been recorded many times. The classic version is the 1955
recording by the great Peter Dawson, backed by the London
Symphony Orchestra conducted by Sir Charles Mackerras.

At this time the floodplains in north-western New South Wales,
around the important tributaries of the Darling, were vast
and fertile. The Paroo Overflow is perhaps the most typical.
It is presumably in this region that Clancy was working.

# AN IDYLL OF DANDALOO

### A.B. *Paterson*

On Western plains, where shade is not,
 'Neath summer skies of cloudless blue,
Where all is dry and all is hot,
 There stands the town of Dandaloo –
A township where life's total sum
Is sleep, diversified with rum.

Its grass-grown streets with dust are deep,
 'Twere vain endeavour to express
The dreamless silence of its sleep,
 Its wide, expansive drunkenness.
The yearly races mostly drew
A lively crowd to Dandaloo.

There came a sportsman from the East,
 The eastern land where sportsmen blow,
And brought with him a speedy beast –
 A speedy beast as horses go.
He came afar in hope to 'do'
The little town of Dandaloo.

Now this was weak of him, I wot –
 Exceeding weak, it seemed to me –
For we in Dandaloo were not

The Jugginses we seemed to be;
In fact, we rather thought we knew
Our book by heart in Dandaloo.

We held a meeting at the bar,
 And met the question fair and square –
'We've stumped the country near and far
 To raise the cash for races here;
We've got a hundred pounds or two –
Not half so bad for Dandaloo.

'And now, it seems, we have to be
 Cleaned out by this here Sydney bloke,
With his imported horse; and he
 Will scoop the pool and leave us broke
Shall we sit still, and make no fuss
While this chap climbs all over us?'

* * *

The races came to Dandaloo,
 And all the cornstalks from the West,
On ev'ry kind of moke and screw,
 Came forth in all their glory drest.
The stranger's horse, as hard as nails,
Look'd fit to run for New South Wales.

He won the race by half a length –
 *Quite* half a length, it seemed to me –

But Dandaloo, with all its strength,
 Roared out 'Dead heat!' most fervently;
And, after hesitation meet,
The judge's verdict was 'Dead heat!'

And many men there were could tell
 What gave the verdict extra force:
The stewards, and the judge as well –
 They all had backed the second horse.
For things like this they sometimes do
In larger towns than Dandaloo.

They ran it off; the stranger won,
 Hands down, by near a hundred yards
He smiled to think his troubles done;
 But Dandaloo held all the cards.
They went to scale and – cruel fate! –
His jockey turned out under-weight.

Perhaps they'd tampered with the scale!
 I cannot tell. I only know
It weighed him *out* all right. I fail
 To paint that Sydney sportsman's woe.
He said the stewards were a crew
Of low-lived thieves in Dandaloo.

He lifted up his voice, irate,
 And swore till all the air was blue;
So then we rose to vindicate
 The dignity of Dandaloo.

'Look here,' said we, 'you must not poke
Such oaths at us poor country folk.'

We rode him softly on a rail,
 We shied at him, in careless glee,
Some large tomatoes, rank and stale,
 And eggs of great antiquity –
Their wild, unholy fragrance flew
About the town of Dandaloo.

He left the town at break of day,
 He led his race-horse through the streets,
And now he tells the tale, they say,
 To every racing man he meets.
And Sydney sportsmen all eschew
The atmosphere of Dandaloo.

Dandaloo features in many personal accounts of Cobb & Co
journeys; passengers stayed at Richardson's Dandaloo Inn
on the banks of the Bogan River. It was linked by stagecoach
tracks to nearby Trangie and Nyngan.

Jugginses = a legendary family of idiots; in recent times, they
seem to have been supplanted in notoriety by the Mugginses
cornstalk = a native-born Australian (those of them who
went off to the Boer War were 'Tommy Cornstalks')
moke and screw = broken-down horses
they ran it off = after the deadheat, there was a 'run-off', a re-run
we rode him softly on a rail = 'riding on a rail' was a traditional
act of humiliation and punishment, but this is the softer
version – a few old eggs and tomatoes hurled in derision

# THE GEEBUNG POLO CLUB

### A.B. *Paterson*

It was somewhere up the country, in a land of rock and scrub,
That they formed an institution called the Geebung Polo Club.
They were long and wiry natives from the rugged mountain side,
And the horse was never saddled that the Geebungs couldn't ride;
But their style of playing polo was irregular and rash –
They had mighty little science, but a mighty lot of dash:
And they played on mountain ponies that were muscular and strong,
Though their coats were quite unpolished, and their manes and tails were long.
And they used to train those ponies wheeling cattle in the scrub:
They were demons, were the members of the Geebung Polo Club.

It was somewhere down the country, in a city's smoke and steam,
That a polo club existed, called 'The Cuff and Collar Team'.
As a social institution 'twas a marvellous success,
For the members were distinguished by exclusiveness and dress.
They had natty little ponies that were nice, and smooth, and sleek,
For their cultivated owners only rode 'em once a week.
So they started up the country in pursuit of sport and fame,
For they meant to show the Geebungs how they ought to play the game;
And they took their valets with them – just to give their boots a rub
Ere they started operations on the Geebung Polo Club.

Now my readers can imagine how the contest ebbed and flowed,
When the Geebung boys got going it was time to clear the road;

And the game was so terrific that ere half the time was gone
A spectator's leg was broken – just from merely looking on.
For they waddied one another till the plain was strewn with dead,
While the score was kept so even that they neither got ahead.
And the Cuff and Collar Captain, when he tumbled off to die,
Was the last surviving player – so the game was called a tie.

Then the Captain of the Geebungs raised him slowly from the ground,
Though his wounds were mostly mortal, yet he fiercely gazed around;
There was no one to oppose him – all the rest were in a trance,
So he scrambled on his pony for his last expiring chance,
For he meant to make an effort to get victory to his side;
So he struck at goal – and missed it – then he tumbled off and died.

\* \* \*

By the old Campaspe River, where the breezes shake the grass,
There's a row of little gravestones that the stockmen never pass,
For they bear a crude inscription saying, 'Stranger, drop a tear,
For the Cuff and Collar players and the Geebung boys lie here.'
And on misty moonlit evenings, while the dingoes howl around,
You can see their shadows flitting down that phantom polo ground;
You can hear the loud collisions as the flying players meet,
And the rattle of the mallets, and the rush of ponies' feet,
Till the terrified spectator rides like blazes to the pub –
He's been haunted by the spectres of the Geebung Polo Club.

---

The Campaspe River meets the Murray at Echuca.

# THE TRAVELLING POST OFFICE

### A.B. Paterson

The roving breezes come and go, the reed beds sweep and sway,
The sleepy river murmurs low, and loiters on its way,
It is the land of lots o' time along the Castlereagh.

\* \* \*

The old man's son had left the farm, he found it dull and slow,
He drifted to the great North-west where all the rovers go.
"He's gone so long," the old man said, "he's dropped right out of mind,
But if you'd write a line to him I'd take it very kind;
He's shearing here and fencing there, a kind of waif and stray,
He's droving now with Conroy's sheep along the Castlereagh.

"The sheep are travelling for the grass, and travelling very slow;
They may be at Mundooran now, or past the Overflow,
Or tramping down the black soil flats across by Waddiwong,
But all those little country towns would send the letter wrong,
The mailman, if he's extra tired, would pass them in his sleep,
It's safest to address the note to 'Care of Conroy's sheep',
For five and twenty thousand head can scarcely go astray,
You write to 'Care of Conroy's sheep along the Castlereagh'."

\* \* \*

By rock and ridge and riverside the western mail has gone,
Across the great Blue Mountain Range to take that letter on.
A moment on the topmost grade while open fire doors glare,
She pauses like a living thing to breathe the mountain air,
Then launches down the other side across the plains away
To bear that note to 'Conroy's sheep along the Castlereagh'.

And now by coach and mailman's bag it goes from town to town,
And Conroy's Gap and Conroy's Creek have marked it 'further down'.
Beneath a sky of deepest blue where never cloud abides,
A speck upon the waste of plain the lonely mailman rides.
Where fierce hot winds have set the pine and myall boughs asweep
He hails the shearers passing by for news of Conroy's sheep.
By big lagoons where wildfowl play and crested pigeons flock,
By camp fires where the drovers ride around their restless stock,
And past the teamster toiling down to fetch the wool away
My letter chases Conroy's sheep along the Castlereagh.

*the western mail* = the mighty steam locomotive that carried
passengers and mail each night over the Blue Mountains
to Lithgow, and beyond to Parkes and Dubbo

# SALTBUSH BILL

### A.B. *Paterson*

Now this is the law of the Overland that all in the West obey,
A man must cover with travelling sheep a six-mile stage a day;
But this is the law which the drovers make, right easily understood,
They travel their stage where the grass is bad, but they camp where the grass is good;
They camp, and they ravage the squatter's grass till never a blade remains,
Then they drift away as the white clouds drift on the edge of the saltbush plains,
From camp to camp and from run to run they battle it hand to hand,
For a blade of grass and the right to pass on the track of the Overland.
For this is the law of the Great Stock Routes, 'tis written in white and black –
The man that goes with a travelling mob must keep to a half-mile track;
And the drovers keep to a half-mile track on the runs where the grass is dead,
But they spread their sheep on a well-grassed run till they go with a two-mile spread.
So the squatters hurry the drovers on from dawn till the fall of night,
And the squatters' dogs and the drovers' dogs get mixed in a deadly fight;
Yet the squatters' men, though they hunt the mob, are willing the peace to keep,
For the drovers learn how to use their hands when they go with the travelling sheep;
But this is the tale of a Jackaroo that came from a foreign strand,
And the fight that he fought with Saltbush Bill, the King of the Overland.

Now Saltbush Bill was a drover tough, as ever the country knew,
He had fought his way on the Great Stock Routes from the sea to the big Barcoo;
He could tell when he came to a friendly run that gave him a chance to spread,
And he knew where the hungry owners were that hurried his sheep ahead;
He was drifting down in the Eighty drought with a mob that could scarcely creep,
(When the kangaroos by the thousands starve, it is rough on the travelling sheep),

And he camped one night at the crossing-place on the edge of the Wilga run,
'We must manage a feed for them here,' he said, 'or the half of the mob are done!'
So he spread them out when they left the camp wherever they liked to go,
Till he grew aware of a Jackaroo with a station-hand in tow,
And they set to work on the straggling sheep, and with many a stockwhip crack
They forced them in where the grass was dead in the space of the half-mile track;
So William prayed that the hand of fate might suddenly strike him blue
But he'd get some grass for his starving sheep in the teeth of that Jackaroo.
So he turned and he cursed the Jackaroo, he cursed him alive or dead,
From the soles of his great unwieldy feet to the crown of his ugly head,
With an extra curse on the moke he rode and the cur at his heels that ran,
Till the Jackaroo from his horse got down and he went for the drover-man;
With the station-hand for his picker-up, though the sheep ran loose the while,
They battled it out on the saltbush plain in the regular prize-ring style.

Now, the new chum fought for his honour's sake and the pride of the English race,
But the drover fought for his daily bread with a smile on his bearded face;
So he shifted ground and he sparred for wind and he made it a lengthy mill,
And from time to time as his scouts came in they whispered to Saltbush Bill –
'We have spread the sheep with a two-mile spread, and the grass it is something grand,
You must stick to him, Bill, for another round for the pride of the Overland.'
The new chum made it a rushing fight, though never a blow got home,
Till the sun rode high in the cloudless sky and glared on the brick-red loam,
Till the sheep drew in to the shelter-trees and settled them down to rest,
Then the drover said he would fight no more and he gave his opponent best.

So the new chum rode to the homestead straight and he told them a story grand
Of the desperate fight that he fought that day with the King of the Overland.
And the tale went home to the Public Schools of the pluck of the English swell,

How the drover fought for his very life, but blood in the end must tell.
But the travelling sheep and the Wilga sheep were boxed on the Old Man Plain.
'Twas a full week's work ere they drafted out and hunted them off again,
With a week's good grass in their wretched hides, with a curse and a stockwhip crack,
They hunted them off on the road once more to starve on the half-mile track.
And Saltbush Bill, on the Overland, will many a time recite
How the best day's work that ever he did was the day that he lost the fight.

Paterson knew first-hand of the ruses drovers adopted to keep their sheep alive. Legally, they had to move their sheep at a rate of six miles a day, and ten miles a day for cattle. They were supposed to keep to a half-mile width but, when they were desperate for good grass, they would allow their sheep to spread further afield and barely move them along at all. The best-known Old Man Plain was between Hay and Deniliquin, in New South Wales's Riverina area.

the Eighty drought = in the early 1880s most of Australia suffered a notoriously severe drought
Jackeroo = virtually a trainee manager and much higher in the pecking order than a station-hand, who held no managerial aspirations
picker-up = normally a rouseabout in the shearing shed, but here meaning a boxer's second

# A MOUNTAIN STATION

### A.B. *Paterson*

I bought a run a while ago,
 On country rough and ridgy,
Where wallaroos and wombats grow –
 The Upper Murrumbidgee.
The grass is rather scant, it's true,
 But this a fair exchange is,
The sheep can see a lovely view
 By climbing up the ranges.

And She-oak Flat's the station's name,
 I'm not surprised at that, sirs:
The oaks were there before I came,
 And I supplied the flat, sirs.
A man would wonder how it's done,
 The stock so soon decreases –
They sometimes tumble off the run
 And break themselves to pieces.

I've tried to make expenses meet,
 But wasted all my labours,
The sheep the dingoes didn't eat
 Were stolen by the neighbours.
They stole my pears – my native pears –
 Those thrice-convicted felons,

And ravished from me unawares
  My crop of paddy-melons.

And sometimes under sunny skies,
  Without an explanation,
The Murrumbidgee used to rise
  And overflow the station.
But this was caused (as now I know)
  When summer sunshine glowing
Had melted all Kiandra's snow
  And set the river going.

And in the news, perhaps you read:
  'Stock passings. Puckawidgee,
Fat cattle: Seven hundred head
  Swept down the Murrumbidgee;
Their destination's quite obscure,
  But, somehow, there's a notion,
Unless the river falls, they're sure
  To reach the Southern Ocean.'

So after that I'll give it best;
  No more with Fate I'll battle.
I'll let the river take the rest,
  For those were all my cattle.
And with one comprehensive curse
  I close my brief narration,
And advertise it in my verse –
  'For Sale! A Mountain Station.'

# THE MAN FROM IRONBARK

### A.B. *Paterson*

It was the man from Ironbark who struck the Sydney town,
He wandered over street and park, he wandered up and down.
He loitered here, he loitered there, till he was like to drop,
Until at last in sheer despair he sought a barber's shop.
"Ere! shave my beard and whiskers off, I'll be a man of mark,
I'll go and do the Sydney toff up home in Ironbark.'

The barber man was small and flash, as barbers mostly are,
He wore a strike-your-fancy sash, he smoked a huge cigar:
He was a humorist of note and keen at repartee,
He laid the odds and kept a 'tote', whatever that may be,
And when he saw our friend arrive, he whispered 'Here's a lark!
Just watch me catch him all alive, this man from Ironbark.'

There were some gilded youths that sat along the barber's wall,
Their eyes were dull, their heads were flat, they had no brains at all;
To them the barber passed the wink, his dexter eyelid shut,
'I'll make this bloomin' yokel think his bloomin' throat is cut.'
And as he soaped and rubbed it in he made a rude remark:
'I s'pose the flats is pretty green up there in Ironbark.'

A grunt was all reply he got; he shaved the bushman's chin,
Then made the water boiling hot and dipped the razor in.
He raised his hand, his brow grew black, he paused awhile to gloat,

Then slashed the red-hot razor-back across his victim's throat;
Upon the newly shaven skin it made a livid mark –
No doubt it fairly took him in – the man from Ironbark.

He fetched a wild up-country yell might wake the dead to hear,
And though his throat, he knew full well, was cut from ear to ear,
He struggled gamely to his feet, and faced the murd'rous foe:
'You've done for me! you dog, I'm beat! one hit before I go!
I only wish I had a knife, you blessed murdering shark!
But you'll remember all your life, the man from Ironbark.'

He lifted up his hairy paw, with one tremendous clout
He landed on the barber's jaw, and knocked the barber out.
He set to work with tooth and nail, he made the place a wreck;
He grabbed the nearest gilded youth, and tried to break his neck.
And all the while his throat he held to save his vital spark,
And 'Murder! Bloody Murder!' yelled the man from Ironbark.

A peeler man who heard the din came in to see the show;
He tried to run the bushman in, but he refused to go.
And when at last the barber spoke, and said, ''Twas all in fun –
'Twas just a little harmless joke, a trifle overdone.'
'A joke!' he cried, 'By George, that's fine; a lively sort of lark;
I'd like to catch that murdering swine some night in Ironbark.'

And now while round the shearing floor the list'ning shearers gape,
He tells the story o'er and o'er, and brags of his escape.
'Them barber chaps what keeps a tote, By George, I've had enough,

One tried to cut my bloomin' throat, but thank the Lord it's tough.'
And whether he's believed or no, there's one thing to remark,
That flowing beards are all the go way up in Ironbark.

---

*peeler* = a policeman in British slang

# LOST

### A.B. *Paterson*

'He ought to be home,' said the old man, 'without there's something amiss.
He only went to the Two-mile – he ought to be back by this.
He would ride the Reckless filly, he would have his wilful way;
And, here, he's not back at sundown – and what will his mother say?

'He was always his mother's idol, since ever his father died;
And there isn't a horse on the station that he isn't game to ride.
But that Reckless mare is vicious, and if once she gets away
He hasn't got strength to hold her – and what will his mother say?'

The old man walked to the sliprail, and peered up the dark'ning track,
And looked and longed for the rider that would never more come back;
And the mother came and clutched him, with sudden, spasmodic fright:
'What has become of my Willie? – why isn't he home to-night?'

Away in the gloomy ranges, at the foot of an ironbark,
The bonnie, winsome laddie was lying stiff and stark;
For the Reckless mare had smashed him against a leaning limb,
And his comely face was battered, and his merry eyes were dim.

And the thoroughbred chestnut filly, the saddle beneath her flanks,
Was away like fire through the ranges to join the wild mob's ranks;
And a broken-hearted woman and an old man worn and grey
Were searching all night in the ranges till the sunrise brought the day.

And the mother kept feebly calling, with a hope that would not die,
'Willie! where are you, Willie?' But how can the dead reply;
And hope died out with the daylight, and the darkness brought despair,
God pity the stricken mother, and answer the widow's prayer!

Though far and wide they sought him, they found not where he fell;
For the ranges held him precious, and guarded their treasure well.
The wattle blooms above him, and the blue bells blow close by,
And the brown bees buzz the secret, and the wild birds sing reply.

But the mother pined and faded, and cried, and took no rest,
And rode each day to the ranges on her hopeless, weary quest.
Seeking her loved one ever, she faded and pined away,
But with strength of her great affection she still sought every day.

'I know that sooner or later I shall find my boy,' she said.
But she came not home one evening, and they found her lying dead,
And stamped on the poor pale features, as the spirit homeward pass'd,
Was an angel smile of gladness – she had found the boy at last.

# A BUSHMAN'S SONG

### A.B. *Paterson*

I'm travellin' down the Castlereagh, and I'm a station hand,
I'm handy with the ropin' pole, I'm handy with the brand,
And I can ride a rowdy colt, or swing the axe all day,
But there's no demand for a station-hand along the Castlereagh.

*So it's shift, boys, shift, for there isn't the slightest doubt*
*That we've got to make a shift to the stations further out,*
*With the pack-horse runnin' after, for he follows like a dog,*
*We must strike across the country at the old jig-jog.*

This old black horse I'm riding – if you'll notice what's his brand,
He wears the crooked R, you see – none better in the land.
He takes a lot of beatin', and the other day we tried,
For a bit of a joke, with a racing bloke, for twenty pounds a side.

*It was shift, boys, shift, for there wasn't the slightest doubt*
*That I had to make him shift, for the money was nearly out;*
*But he cantered home a winner, with the other one at the flog –*
*He's a red-hot sort to pick up with his old jig-jog.*

I asked a cove for shearin' once along the Marthaguy:
'We shear non-union here,' says he. 'I call it scab,' says I.
I looked along the shearin' floor before I turned to go –
There were eight or ten dashed Chinamen a-shearin' in a row.

*It was shift, boys, shift, for there wasn't the slightest doubt*
*It was time to make a shift with the leprosy about.*
*So I saddled up my horses, and I whistled to my dog,*
*And I left his scabby station at the old jig-jog.*

I went to Illawarra, where my brother's got a farm,
He has to ask his landlord's leave before he lifts his arm;
The landlord owns the country side – man, woman, dog, and cat,
They haven't the cheek to dare to speak without they touch their hat.

*It was shift, boys, shift, for there wasn't the slightest doubt*
*Their little landlord god and I would soon have fallen out;*
*Was I to touch my hat to him? – was I his bloomin' dog?*
*So I makes for up the country at the old jig-jog.*

But it's time that I was movin', I've a mighty way to go
Till I drink artesian water from a thousand feet below;
Till I meet the overlanders with the cattle comin' down,
And I'll work a while till I make a pile, then have a spree in town.

*So, it's shift, boys, shift, for there isn't the slightest doubt*
*We've got to make a shift to the stations further out;*
*The pack-horse runs behind us, for he follows like a dog,*
*And we cross a lot of country at the old jig-jog.*

# A BUSH CHRISTENING

## A.B. *Paterson*

On the outer Barcoo where the churches are few,
 And men of religion are scanty,
On a road never cross'd 'cept by folk that are lost,
 One Michael Magee had a shanty.

Now this Mike was the dad of a ten year old lad,
 Plump, healthy, and stoutly conditioned;
He was strong as the best, but poor Mike had no rest
 For the youngster had never been christened.

And his wife used to cry, 'If the darlin' should die
 Saint Peter would not recognise him.'
But by luck he survived till a preacher arrived,
 Who agreed straightaway to baptise him.

Now the artful young rogue, while they held their collogue,
 With his ear to the keyhole was listenin',
And he muttered in fright, while his features turned white,
 'What the divil and all is this christenin'?'

He was none of your dolts, he had seen them brand colts,
 And it seemed to his small understanding,
If the man in the frock made him one of the flock,
 It must mean something very like branding.

So away with a rush he set off for the bush,
  While the tears in his eyelids they glistened –
''Tis outrageous,' says he, 'to brand youngsters like me,
  I'll be dashed if I'll stop to be christened!'

Like a young native dog he ran into a log,
  And his father with language uncivil,
Never heeding the 'praste' cried aloud in his haste,
  'Come out and be christened, you divil!'

But he lay there as snug as a bug in a rug,
  And his parents in vain might reprove him,
Till his reverence spoke (he was fond of a joke)
  'I've a notion,' says he, 'that'll move him.'

'Poke a stick up the log, give the spalpeen a prog;
  Poke him aisy – don't hurt him or maim him,
'Tis not long that he'll stand, I've the water at hand,
  As he rushes out this end I'll name him.

'Here he comes, and for shame! ye've forgotten the name –
  Is it Patsy or Michael or Dinnis?'
Here the youngster ran out, and the priest gave a shout –
  'Take your chance, anyhow, wid 'Maginnis'!'

As the howling young cub ran away to the scrub
  Where he knew that pursuit would be risky,
The priest, as he fled, flung a flask at his head
  That was labelled 'MAGINNIS'S WHISKY'!

And Maginnis Magee has been made a J.P.,
 And the one thing he hates more than sin is
To be asked by the folk, who have heard of the joke,
 How he came to be christened 'Maginnis'!

---

*spalpeen* = the Irish description of a good-for-nothing
*prog* = a progue; that is, a sharp point

# MULGA BILL'S BICYCLE

### A.B. *Paterson*

'Twas Mulga Bill, from Eaglehawk, that caught the cycling craze;
He turned away the good old horse that served him many days;
He dressed himself in cycling clothes, resplendent to be seen;
He hurried off to town and bought a shining new machine;
And as he wheeled it through the door, with air of lordly pride,
The grinning shop assistant said, 'Excuse me, can you ride?'

'See, here, young man,' said Mulga Bill, 'from Walgett to the sea,
From Conroy's Gap to Castlereagh, there's none can ride like me.
I'm good all round at everything, as everybody knows,
Although I'm not the one to talk – I *hate* a man that blows.
But riding is my special gift, my chiefest, sole delight;
Just ask a wild duck can it swim, a wild cat can it fight.
There's nothing clothed in hair or hide, or built of flesh or steel,
There's nothing walks or jumps, or runs, on axle, hoof, or wheel,
But what I'll sit, while hide will hold and girths and straps are tight:
I'll ride this here two-wheeled concern right straight away at sight.'

'Twas Mulga Bill, from Eaglehawk, that sought his own abode,
That perched above the Dead Man's Creek, beside the mountain road.
He turned the cycle down the hill and mounted for the fray,
But 'ere he'd gone a dozen yards it bolted clean away.
It left the track, and through the trees, just like a silver streak,
It whistled down the awful slope, towards the Dead Man's Creek.

It shaved a stump by half an inch, it dodged a big white-box:
The very wallaroos in fright went scrambling up the rocks,
The wombats hiding in their caves dug deeper underground,
As Mulga Bill, as white as chalk, sat tight to every bound.
It struck a stone and gave a spring that cleared a fallen tree,
It raced beside a precipice as close as close could be;
And then as Mulga Bill let out one last despairing shriek
It made a leap of twenty feet into the Dead Man's Creek.

'Twas Mulga Bill, from Eaglehawk, that slowly swam ashore:
He said, 'I've had some narrer shaves and lively rides before;
I've rode a wild bull round a yard to win a five pound bet,
But this was the most awful ride that I've encountered yet.
I'll give that two-wheeled outlaw best; it's shaken all my nerve
To feel it whistle through the air and plunge and buck and swerve.
It's safe at rest in Dead Man's Creek, we'll leave it lying still;
A horse's back is good enough henceforth for Mulga Bill.'

---

Eaglehawk was a former gold-mining town in Victoria, but
today it is a suburb within the City of Greater Bendigo.
Inevitably, it boasts a Mulga Bill Bicycle Trail, taking in
many of the mining attractions and historic sites.

# SONG OF THE ARTESIAN WATER

### A.B. Paterson

Now the stock have started dying, for the Lord has sent a drought;
But we're sick of prayers and Providence – we're going to do without;
With the derricks up above us and the solid earth below,
We are waiting at the lever for the word to let her go.

*Sinking down, deeper down,*
*Oh, we'll sink it deeper down:*
*As the drill is plugging downward at a thousand feet of level,*
*If the Lord won't send us water, oh, we'll get it from the devil;*
*Yes, we'll get it from the devil deeper down.*

Now, our engine's built in Glasgow by a very canny Scot,
And he marked it twenty horse-power, but he don't know what is what:
When Canadian Bill is firing with the sun-dried gidgee logs,
She can equal thirty horses and a score or so of dogs.

*Sinking down, deeper down,*
*Oh, we're going deeper down:*
*If we fail to get the water then it's ruin to the squatter,*
*For the drought is on the station and the weather's growing hotter,*
*But we're bound to get the water deeper down.*

But the shaft has started caving and the sinking's very slow,
And the yellow rods are bending in the water down below,

And the tubes are always jamming and they can't be made to shift
Till we nearly burst the engine with a forty horse-power lift.

*Sinking down, deeper down,*
*Oh, we're going deeper down*
*Though the shaft is always caving, and the tubes are always jamming,*
*Yet we'll fight our way to water while the stubborn drill is ramming –*
*While the stubborn drill is ramming deeper down.*

But there's no artesian water, though we've passed three thousand feet,
And the contract price is growing and the boss is nearly beat.
But it must be down beneath us, and it's down we've got to go,
Though she's bumping on the solid rock four thousand feet below.

*Sinking down, deeper down,*
*Oh, we're going deeper down:*
*And it's time they heard us knocking on the roof of Satan's dwellin';*
*But we'll get artesian water if we cave the roof of hell in –*
*Oh! we'll get artesian water deeper down.*

But it's hark! the whistle's blowing with a wild, exultant blast,
And the boys are madly cheering, for they've struck the flow at last,
And it's rushing up the tubing from four thousand feet below
Till it spouts above the casing in a million-gallon flow.

*And it's down, deeper down –*
*Oh, it comes from deeper down;*
*It is flowing, ever flowing, in a free, unstinted measure*
*From the silent hidden places where the old earth hides her treasure –*
*Where the old earth hides her treasure deeper down.*

And it's clear away the timber, and it's let the water run:
How it glimmers in the shadow, how it flashes in the sun!
By the silent belts of timber, by the miles of blazing plain
It is bringing hope and comfort to the thirsty land again.

*Flowing down, further down;*
*It is flowing further down*
*To the tortured thirsty cattle, bringing gladness in its going;*
*Through the droughty days of summer it is flowing, ever flowing –*
*It is flowing, ever flowing, further down.*

# THE ROAD TO GUNDAGAI

### A.B. *Paterson*

The mountain road goes up and down,
From Gundagai to Tumut Town.

And branching off there runs a track,
Across the foothills grim and black,

Across the plains and ranges grey
To Sydney city far away.

\* \* \*

It came by chance one day that I
From Tumut rode to Gundagai.

And reached about the evening tide
The crossing where the roads divide;

And, waiting at the crossing place,
I saw a maiden fair of face,

With eyes of deepest violet blue,
And cheeks to match the rose in hue –

The fairest maids Australia knows
Are bred among the mountain snows.

Then, fearing I might go astray,
I asked if she could show the way.

Her voice might well a man bewitch –
Its tones so supple, deep, and rich.

'The tracks are clear,' she made reply,
'And this goes down to Sydney town,
And that one goes to Gundagai.'

Then slowly, looking coyly back,
She went along the Sydney track.

And I for one was well content
To go the road the lady went;

But round the turn a swain she met –
The kiss she gave him haunts me yet!

\* \* \*

I turned and travelled with a sigh
The lonely road to Gundagai.

---

It has been suggested that this poem tells in code of
a romantic encounter between Miles Franklin (very
much a daughter of Tumut) and The Banjo, whose
heartland was in the Yass/Gundagai area.

# WALTZING MATILDA

## A.B. *Paterson*

Oh! there once was a swagman camped in the Billabong,
 Under the shade of a Coolabah tree;
And he sang as he looked at his old billy boiling,
 "Who'll come a-waltzing Matilda with me."

 Who'll come a-waltzing Matilda, my darling,
  Who'll come a-waltzing Matilda with me?
 Waltzing Matilda and leading a water-bag –
  Who'll come a-waltzing Matilda with me?

Down came a jumbuck to drink at the water-hole,
 Up jumped the swagman and grabbed him in glee;
And he sang as he put him away in his tucker-bag,
 "You'll come a-waltzing Matilda with me!"

Down came the Squatter a-riding his thorough-bred;
 Down came Policemen – one, two, and three.
"Whose is the jumbuck you've got in the tucker-bag?
 You'll come a-waltzing Matilda with me."

But the swagman, he up and he jumped in the water-hole,
 Drowning himself by the Coolabah tree;
And his ghost may be heard as it sings in the Billabong,
 "Who'll come a-waltzing Matilda with me?"

There are many variants of this famous ballad, but this is how it was first published in Paterson's collection, *Saltbush Bill J.P. and Other Verses*, in 1917. The ballad bore the subtitle 'Carrying a swag' to explain the meaning of the title, which indicates it was not a widely known term at that time.

Indisputably it was written in 1895, while Paterson was staying at Dagworth Homestead near Winton in Queensland. It was probably inspired by events that occurred towards the end of the 1891 Great Shearers Strike, when the owner of Dagworth and three policemen chased a man called Samuel Hoffmeister, who, rather than be captured, opted to shoot himself at the Combo Waterhole. There is considerable argument as to where Paterson's sympathies lay in this matter, but it is unlikely that it was composed as a socialist anthem.

In 1903 it was licensed to the Billy Tea company for use as an advertising jingle, making it nationally famous. The poet later sold the rights in 'Waltzing Matilda' and 'some other pieces' to Angus & Robertson for five pounds, perhaps not foreseeing their future popularity. It is the most recognisable Australian song and could fairly be described as ubiquitous. It has been recorded many times and with many musical settings. For better or for worse, it has inspired both the great and the not-so-great.

# HENRY LAWSON
## (1867–1922)

When Sydney's George Robertson, the canny proprietor of the Angus & Robertson bookshop, began to dabble in publishing, he quickly took note of the popularity of the writing of Banjo Paterson and Henry Lawson in *The Bulletin*. Having launched Paterson's first collection in 1895 with great commercial success, he published a collection of Lawson's verse (*In the Days When the World Was Wide*) in February 1896 and followed that up with a collection of his short stories (*While the Billy Boils*) six months later.

Lawson's short stories are generally rated by scholars as superior to his verse and considered to be a major contribution to Australian literature. However, his verse was hugely popular in his lifetime and continues to be so today, even if over-shadowed by Paterson. In contrast to the infectious exuberance and romanticism of The Banjo, Lawson's verse offers a wistful nostalgia – he recognised that the great pioneering days were over and mourned their passing. As a committed socialist, he was concerned for the well-being of those who had drifted to the growing cities and had failed to prosper there.

Three years younger that Paterson, Lawson was doomed to lead a shorter and less stable life. He was born on the New

South Wales goldfields; but his father, a Norwegian-born miner, and his mother, the influential feminist Louisa Lawson, soon recognised their utter incompatibility. In time Henry married the daughter of a famous socialist bookseller, but this too proved an unhappy match. The legendary NSW Labor premier, J.T. Lang, was his brother-in-law.

For a great deal of his life, Lawson fought a battle against alcoholism and depression. He happily cadged money off both friends and strangers. He was imprisoned in Darlinghurst Gaol for drunkenness and non-payment of alimony – he referred to it as 'Starvinghurst Gaol' because of the meagre rations given to the inmates. And yet when he died he was accorded a state funeral, which was attended by the Australian prime minister of the day, Billy Hughes, plus the NSW premier and many thousands of the poet's admiring fellow citizens.

# FACES IN THE STREET

*Henry Lawson*

They lie, the men who tell us in a loud decisive tone
That want is here a stranger, and that misery's unknown;
For where the nearest suburb and the city proper meet
My window-sill is level with the faces in the street –
Drifting past, drifting past,
To the beat of weary feet –
While I sorrow for the owners of those faces in the street.

And cause I have to sorrow, in a land so young and fair,
To see upon those faces stamped the marks of Want and Care;
I look in vain for traces of the fresh and fair and sweet
In sallow, sunken faces that are drifting through the street –
Drifting on, drifting on,
To the scrape of restless feet;
I can sorrow for the owners of the faces in the street.

In hours before the dawning dims the starlight in the sky
The wan and weary faces first begin to trickle by,
Increasing as the moments hurry on with morning feet,
Till like a pallid river flow the faces in the street –
Flowing in, flowing in,
To the beat of hurried feet –
Ah! I sorrow for the owners of those faces in the street.

The human river dwindles when 'tis past the hour of eight,
Its waves go flowing faster in the fear of being late;
But slowly drag the moments, whilst beneath the dust and heat
The city grinds the owners of the faces in the street –
Grinding body, grinding soul,
Yielding scarce enough to eat –
Oh! I sorrow for the owners of the faces in the street.

And then the only faces till the sun is sinking down
Are those of outside toilers and the idlers of the town,
Save here and there a face that seems a stranger in the street,
Tells of the city's unemployed upon his weary beat –
Drifting round, drifting round,
To the tread of listless feet –
Ah! My heart aches for the owner of that sad face in the street.

And when the hours on lagging feet have slowly dragged away,
And sickly yellow gaslights rise to mock the going day,
Then flowing past my window like a tide in its retreat,
Again I see the pallid stream of faces in the street –
Ebbing out, ebbing out,
To the drag of tired feet,
While my heart is aching dumbly for the faces in the street.

And now all blurred and smirched with vice the day's sad pages end,
For while the short 'large hours' toward the longer 'small hours' trend,
With smiles that mock the wearer, and with words that half entreat,
Delilah pleads for custom at the corner of the street –
Sinking down, sinking down,

Battered wreck by tempests beat –
A dreadful, thankless trade is hers, that Woman of the Street.

But, ah! to dreader things than these our fair young city comes,
For in its heart are growing thick the filthy dens and slums,
Where human forms shall rot away in sties for swine unmeet,
And ghostly faces shall be seen unfit for any street –
Rotting out, rotting out,
For the lack of air and meat –
In dens of vice and horror that are hidden from the street.

I wonder would the apathy of wealthy men endure
Were all their windows level with the faces of the Poor?
Ah! Mammon's slaves, your knees shall knock, your hearts in terror beat,
When God demands a reason for the sorrows of the street,
The wrong things and the bad things
And the sad things that we meet
In the filthy lane and alley, and the cruel, heartless street.

I left the dreadful corner where the steps are never still,
And sought another window overlooking gorge and hill;
But when the night came dreary with the driving rain and sleet,
They haunted me – the shadows of those faces in the street,
Flitting by, flitting by,
Flitting by with noiseless feet,
And with cheeks but little paler than the real ones in the street.

Once I cried: 'Oh, God Almighty! if Thy might doth still endure,
Now show me in a vision for the wrongs of Earth a cure.'

And, lo! with shops all shuttered I beheld a city's street,
And in the warning distance heard the tramp of many feet,
Coming near, coming near,
To a drum's dull distant beat,
And soon I saw the army that was marching down the street.

Then, like a swollen river that has broken bank and wall,
The human flood came pouring with the red flags over all,
And kindled eyes all blazing bright with revolution's heat,
And flashing swords reflecting rigid faces in the street.
Pouring on, pouring on,
To a drum's loud threatening beat,
And the war-hymns and the cheering of the people in the street.

And so it must be while the world goes rolling round its course,
The warning pen shall write in vain, the warning voice grow hoarse,
But not until a city feels Red Revolution's feet
Shall its sad people miss awhile the terrors of the street –
The dreadful everlasting strife
For scarcely clothes and meat
In that pent track of living death – the city's cruel street.

# THE ROARING DAYS

### *Henry Lawson*

The night too quickly passes
And we are growing old,
So let us fill our glasses
And toast the Days of Gold;
When finds of wondrous treasure
Set all the South ablaze,
And you and I were faithful mates
All through the roaring days!

Then stately ships came sailing
From every harbour's mouth,
And sought the land of promise
That beaconed in the South;
Then southward streamed their streamers
And swelled their canvas full
To speed the wildest dreamers
E'er borne in vessel's hull.

Their shining Eldorado,
Beneath the southern skies,
Was day and night for ever
Before their eager eyes.
The brooding bush, awakened,

Was stirred in wild unrest,
And all the year a human stream
Went pouring to the West.

The rough bush roads re-echoed
The bar-room's noisy din,
When troops of stalwart horsemen
Dismounted at the inn.
And oft the hearty greetings
And hearty clasp of hands
Would tell of sudden meetings
Of friends from other lands;
When, puzzled long, the new-chum
Would recognise at last,
Behind a bronzed and bearded skin,
A comrade of the past.

And when the cheery camp-fire
Explored the bush with gleams,
The camping-grounds were crowded
With caravans of teams;
Then home the jests were driven,
And good old songs were sung,
And choruses were given
The strength of heart and lung.
Oh, they were lion-hearted
Who gave our country birth!
Oh, they were of the stoutest sons
From all the lands on earth!

Oft when the camps were dreaming,
And fires began to pale,
Through rugged ranges gleaming
Would come the Royal Mail.
Behind six foaming horses,
And lit by flashing lamps,
Old 'Cobb and Co.'s', in royal state,
Went dashing past the camps.

Oh, who would paint a goldfield,
And limn the picture right,
As we have often seen it
In early morning's light;
The yellow mounds of mullock
With spots of red and white,
The scattered quartz that glistened
Like diamonds in light;
The azure line of ridges,
The bush of darkest green,
The little homes of calico
That dotted all the scene.

I hear the fall of timber
From distant flats and fells,
The pealing of the anvils
As clear as little bells,
The rattle of the cradle,
The clack of windlass-boles,

The flutter of the crimson flags
Above the golden holes.

* * *

Ah, then our hearts were bolder,
And if Dame Fortune frowned
Our swags we'd lightly shoulder
And tramp to other ground.
But golden days are vanished,
And altered is the scene;
The diggings are deserted,
The camping-grounds are green;
The flaunting flag of progress
Is in the West unfurled,
The mighty bush with iron rails
Is tethered to the world.

---

*limn* = to draw or paint
*windlass-bole* = a device Lawson also mentions in his short
stories, but its meaning is hard to divine. The windlass
was used in mining to bring excavated material to the
surface. Rope or cable was wound around a horizontal
cylinder (the barrel), which was turned to raise the bucket.
Possibly a tree's bole (the lowest and thickest part of its
trunk) was sometimes used as a crude windlass barrel.

# ANDY'S GONE WITH CATTLE

### Henry Lawson

Our Andy's gone to battle now
'Gainst Drought, the red marauder;
Our Andy's gone with cattle now
Across the Queensland border.

He's left us in dejection now;
Our hearts with him are roving.
It's dull on this selection now,
Since Andy went a-droving.

Who now shall wear the cheerful face
In times when things are slackest?
And who shall whistle round the place
When Fortune frowns her blackest?

Oh, who shall cheek the squatter now
When he comes round us snarling?
His tongue is growing hotter now
Since Andy cross'd the Darling.

The gates are out of order now,
In storms the 'riders' rattle;
For far across the border now
Our Andy's gone with cattle.

Poor Aunty's looking thin and white;
And Uncle's cross with worry;
And poor old Blucher howls all night
Since Andy left Macquarie.

Oh, may the showers in torrents fall,
And all the tanks run over;
And may the grass grow green and tall
In pathways of the drover;

And may good angels send the rain
On desert stretches sandy;
And when the summer comes again
God grant 'twill bring us Andy.

---

*riders* = timber laid on a bark hut's roof, to secure it
against a high wind

# MIDDLETON'S ROUSEABOUT

### *Henry Lawson*

Tall and feckled and sandy,
Face of a country lout;
This was the picture of Andy,
Middleton's Rouseabout.

Type of a coming nation,
In the land of cattle and sheep,
Worked on Middleton's station,
"Pound a week and his keep".

On Middleton's wide dominions
Plied the stockwhip an' shears;
Hadn't any opinions,
Hadn't any "idears".

Swiftly the years went over,
Liquor and drouth prevailed;
Middleton went as a drover,
After his station had failed.

Type of a careless nation,
Men who are soon played out,
Middleton was – and his station
Was bought by the Rouseabout.

Flourishing beard and sandy,
Tall and robust and stout;
This is the picture of Andy,
Middleton's Rouseabout.

Now on his own dominions
Works with his overseers;
Hasn't any opinions,
Hasn't any "idears".

---

*drouth* = archaic word for drought

# BALLAD OF THE DROVER

*Henry Lawson*

Across the stony ridges,
Across the rolling plain,
Young Harry Dale, the drover,
Comes riding home again.
And well his stock-horse bears him,
And light of heart is he,
And stoutly his old pack-horse
Is trotting by his knee.

Up Queensland way with cattle
He travelled regions vast;
And many months have vanished
Since home-folk saw him last.
He hums a song of someone
He hopes to marry soon;
And hobble-chains and camp-ware
Keep jingling to the tune.

Beyond the hazy dado
Against the lower skies
And yon blue line of ranges
The homestead station lies.
And thitherward the drover
Jogs through the lazy noon,

While hobble-chains and camp-ware
Are jingling to a tune.

An hour has filled the heavens
With storm-clouds inky black;
At times the lightning trickles
Around the drover's track;
But Harry pushes onward,
His horses' strength he tries,
In hope to reach the river
Before the flood shall rise.

The thunder from above him
Goes rolling o'er the plain;
And down on thirsty pastures
In torrents falls the rain.
And every creek and gully
Sends forth its little flood,
Till the river runs a banker,
All stained with yellow mud.

Now Harry speaks to Rover,
The best dog on the plains,
And to his hardy horses,
And strokes their shaggy manes;
'We've breasted bigger rivers
When floods were at their height
Nor shall this gutter stop us
From getting home to-night!'

The thunder growls a warning,
The ghastly lightnings gleam,
As the drover turns his horses
To swim the fatal stream.
But, oh! the flood runs stronger
Than e'er it ran before;
The saddle-horse is failing,
And only half-way o'er!

When flashes next the lightning,
The flood's grey breast is blank,
And a cattle dog and pack-horse
Are struggling up the bank.
But in the lonely homestead
The girl will wait in vain –
He'll never pass the stations
In charge of stock again.

The faithful dog a moment
Sits panting on the bank,
And then swims through the current
To where his master sank.
And round and round in circles
He fights with failing strength,
Till, borne down by the waters,
The old dog sinks at length.

Across the flooded lowlands
And slopes of sodden loam

The pack-horse struggles onward,
To take dumb tidings home.
And mud-stained, wet, and weary,
Through ranges dark goes he;
While hobble-chains and tinware
Are sounding eerily.

* * *

The floods are in the ocean,
The stream is clear again,
And now a verdant carpet
Is stretched across the plain.
But someone's eyes are saddened,
And someone's heart still bleeds
In sorrow for the drover
Who sleeps among the reeds.

---

*dado* = indoors, it is the part of a wall that lies below the
picture rail; metaphorically, it is the low horizon

# THE SONG OF OLD JOE SWALLOW

### Henry Lawson

When I was up the country in the rough and early days,
I used to work along ov Jimmy Nowlett's bullick-drays;
Then the reelroad wasn't heered on, an' the bush was wild an' strange,
An' we useter draw the timber from the saw-pits in the range –
Load provisions for the stations, an' we'd travel far and slow
Through the plains an' 'cross the ranges in the days of long ago.

> *Then it's yoke up the bullicks and tramp beside 'em slow,*
> *An' saddle up yer horses an' a-ridin' we will go,*
> *To the bullick-drivin', cattle-drovin',*
> *Nigger, digger, roarin', rovin'*
> *Days o' long ago.*

Once me and Jimmy Nowlett loaded timber for the town,
But we hadn't gone a dozen mile before the rain come down,
An' me an' Jimmy Nowlett an' the bullicks an' the dray
Was cut off on some risin' ground while floods around us lay;
An' we soon run short of tucker an' terbaccer, which was bad,
An' pertaters dipped in honey was the only tuck we had.

An' half our bullicks perished when the drought was on the land,
An' the burnin' heat that dazzles as it dances on the sand;

141

When the sun-baked clay an' gravel paves for miles the burnin' creeks,
An' at ev'ry step yer travel there a rottin' carcase reeks –
But we pulled ourselves together, for we never used ter know
What a feather bed was good for in those days o' long ago.

But in spite ov barren ridges an' in spite ov mud an' heat,
An' the dust that browned the bushes when it rose from bullicks' feet,
An' in spite ov cold and chilblains when the bush was white with frost,
An' in spite of muddy water where the burnin' plain was crossed,
An' in spite of modern progress, and in spite of all their blow,
'Twas a better land to live in, in the days o' long ago.

When the frosty moon was shinin' o'er the ranges like a lamp,
An' a lot of bullick-drivers was a-campin' on the camp.
When the fire was blazin' cheery an' the pipes was drawin' well,
Then our songs we useter chorus an' our yarns we useter tell,
An' we'd talk ov lands we come from, and ov chaps we useter know
For there always was behind us *other* days o' long ago.

Ah, them early days was ended when the reelroad crossed the plain,
But in dreams I often tramp beside the bullick-team again:
Still we pauses at the shanty just to have a drop er cheer,
Still I feels a kind ov pleasure when the campin'-ground is near;
Still I smells the old tarpaulin me an' Jimmy useter throw
'Cross the timber-truck for shelter in the days ov long ago.

I have been a-driftin' back'ards with the changes ov the land,
An' if I spoke ter bullicks now they wouldn't understand,
But when Mary wakes me sudden in the night, I'll often say:

'Come here, Spot, an' stan' up, Bally, blank an' blank an' come-eer-way.'
An' she says that, when I'm sleepin', oft my elerquince 'ill flow
In the bullick-drivin' language ov the days o' long ago.

Well, the pub will soon be closin', so I'll give the thing a rest;
But if you should drop on Nowlett in the far an' distant west –
An' if Jimmy uses doubleyou instead of ar an' vee,
An' if he drops his aitches, then you're sure to know it's he.
An' yer won't forgit to arsk him if he still remembers Joe
As knowed him up the country in the days o' long ago.

*Then it's yoke up the bullicks and tramp beside 'em slow,*
*An' saddle up yer horses an' a-ridin' we will go,*
*To the bullick-drivin', cattle-drovin',*
*Nigger, digger, roarin', rovin'*
*Days o' long ago.*

# THE LIGHTS OF COBB & CO

## *Henry Lawson*

Fire lighted, on the table a meal for sleepy men,
A lantern in the stable, a jingle now and then;
The mail coach looming darkly by light of moon and star,
The growl of sleepy voices – a candle in the bar.
A stumble in the passage of folk with wits abroad;
A swear-word from a bedroom – the shout of 'All aboard!'
'Tchk-tchk! Git-up!' 'Hold fast, there!' and down the range we go;
Five hundred miles of scattered camps will watch for Cobb and Co.

Old coaching towns already 'decaying for their sins,'
Uncounted 'Half-Way Houses', and scores of 'Ten Mile Inns';
The riders from the stations by lonely granite peaks;
The black-boy for the shepherds on sheep and cattle creeks;
The roaring camps of Gulgong, and many a 'Digger's Rest';
The diggers on the Lachlan; the huts of Farthest West;
Some twenty thousand exiles who sailed for weal or woe;
The bravest hearts of twenty lands will wait for Cobb and Co.

The morning star has vanished, the frost and fog are gone,
In one of those grand mornings which but on mountains dawn;
A flask of friendly whisky – each other's hopes we share –
And throw our top-coats open to drink the mountain air.
The roads are rare to travel, and life seems all complete;
The grind of wheels on gravel, the trot of horses' feet,

The trot, trot, trot and canter, as down the spur we go –
The green sweeps to horizons blue that call for Cobb and Co.

We take a bright girl actress through western dust and damps,
To bear the home-world message, and sing for sinful camps
To wake the hearts and break them, wild hearts that hope and ache –
(Ah! when she thinks of those days her own must nearly break!)
Five miles this side the gold-field, a loud, triumphant shout:
Five hundred cheering diggers have snatched the horses out:
With 'Auld Lang Syne' in chorus through roaring camps they go –
That cheer for her, and cheer for Home, and cheer for Cobb and Co.

Three lamps above the ridges and gorges dark and deep,
A flash on sandstone cuttings where sheer the sidings sweep,
A flash on shrouded waggons, on water ghastly white;
Weird bush and scattered remnants of rushes in the night
Across the swollen river a flash beyond the ford:
'Ride hard to warn the driver! He's drunk or mad, good Lord!'
But on the bank to westward a broad, triumphant glow –
A hundred miles shall see to-night the lights of Cobb and Co.!

Swift scramble up the siding where teams climb inch by inch;
Pause, bird-like, on the summit – then breakneck down the pinch
Past haunted half-way houses – where convicts made the bricks –
Scrub-yards and new bark shanties, we dash with five and six –
By clear, ridge-country rivers, and gaps where tracks run high,
Where waits the lonely horseman, cut clear against the sky;
Through stringy-bark and blue-gum, and box and pine we go;
New camps are stretching 'cross the plains the routes of Cobb and Co.

\* \* \*

Throw down the reins, old driver – there's no one left to shout;
The ruined inn's survivor must take the horses out.
A poor old coach hereafter! – we're lost to all such things –
No bursts of songs or laughter shall shake your leathern springs
When creeping in unnoticed by railway sidings drear,
Or left in yards for lumber, decaying with the year –
Oh, who'll think how in those days when distant fields were broad
You raced across the Lachlan side with twenty-five on board.

Not all the ships that sail away since Roaring Days are done –
Not all the boats that steam from port, nor all the trains that run,
Shall take such hopes and loyal hearts – for men shall never know
Such days as when the Royal Mail was run by Cobb and Co.
The 'greyhounds' race across the sea, the 'special' cleaves the haze,
But these seem dull and slow to me compared with Roaring Days!
The eyes that watched are dim with age, and souls are weak and slow,
The hearts are dust or hardened now that broke for Cobb and Co.

# THE BULLETIN'S
# BACKBLOCK BARDS

*The Bulletin, The Bulletin,*
*The journalistic Javelin,*
*The paper all the humor's in*
*The paper every rumor's in*
*The paper to inspire a grin*
*The Bulletin, The Bulletin*

On 31 January 1880, a new weekly paper was launched by two Sydney journalists, J.F. Archibald and John Haynes. The more prominent of the two was the man born John Feltham Archibald in Kildare (these days Geelong West), who subsequently, in a characteristically quixotic gesture, changed his name to Jules François Archibald out of his infatuation with French culture. At his death, Archibald left two great legacies – Sydney's Archibald Fountain in Hyde Park and the great national art prize for portraiture named in his honour.

*The Bulletin* was destined to become the most famous and the most influential magazine ever published in Australia. It was a time when our culture and our political institutions were in the process of being shaped and *The Bulletin* was humorous, jingoistic, republican, anti-religious and racist, famously running the provocative slogan 'Australia for the White Man' under its masthead (until 1961, when it was removed by its then editor, Donald Horne). Its abiding exuberance is well captured by the self-advertising doggerel reproduced here and published in its pages on 28 May 1887.

Its scathing eye for any signs of pretention, its blokey mateship and its passionate support for the working man quickly won it support everywhere, but particularly beyond the cities. It became known as 'The Bushman's Bible' and by 1900 its circulation had reached 80,000. One of Archibald's acts of genius was to open its pages to its readers, who avidly contributed poetry, short stories, gossip, jokes and cartoons.

Under the guidance of its successive editors and, later, of its influential literary editor, A.G. Stephens, it created and sustained a core stable of writers, of whom Lawson and Paterson were merely the best loved. Most of these (men, predominantly) had been born in the 1860s. Their heyday was, of course, the 1880s, but by the end of the 1890s they began to lose their radical bravura.

# WHERE THE DEAD MEN LIE

### Barcroft Boake

Out on the wastes of the Never Never –
That's where the dead men lie!
There where the heat-waves dance for ever –
That's where the dead men lie!
That's where the Earth's loved sons are keeping
Endless tryst: not the west wind sweeping
Feverish pinions, can wake their sleeping –
Out where the dead men lie!

Where brown Summer and Death have mated –
That's where the dead men lie!
Loving with fiery lust unsated –
That's where the dead men lie!
Out where the grinning skulls bleach whitely
Under the saltbush sparkling brightly;
Out where the wild dogs chorus nightly –
That's where the dead men lie!

Deep in the yellow, flowing river –
That's where the dead men lie!
Under the banks where the shadows quiver –
That's where the dead men lie!
Where the platypus twists and doubles,
Leaving a train of tiny bubbles;

Rid at last of their earthly troubles –
That's where the dead men lie!

East and backward pale faces turning,
That's how the dead men lie!
Gaunt arms stretched with a voiceless yearning –
That's how the dead men lie!
Oft in the fragrant hush of nooning
Hearing again their mothers' crooning,
Wrapt for aye in a dreadful swooning –
That's how the dead men lie!

Only the hand of Night can free them –
That's when the dead men fly!
Only the frightened cattle see them –
See the dead men go by;
Cloven hoofs beating out one measure,
Bidding the stockman know no leisure –
That's when the dead men take their pleasure!
That's when the dead men fly!

Ask, too, the never-sleeping drover:
He sees the dead pass by;
Hearing them call to their friends – the plover,
Hearing the dead men cry;
Seeing their faces stealing, stealing,
Hearing their laughter pealing, pealing,
Watching their grey forms wheeling, wheeling
Round where the cattle lie!

Strangled by thirst and fierce privation –
That's how the dead men die!
Out on Moneygrub's farthest station –
That's how the dead men die!
Hardfaced greybeards, youngsters callow;
Some mounds cared for, some left fallow;
Some deep down, yet others shallow;
Some having but the sky.

Moneygrub, as he sips his claret,
Looks with complacent eye
Down at his watch-chain, eighteen-carat –
There, in his club, hard by:
Recks not that every link is stamped with
Names of the men whose limbs are cramped with
Too long lying in grave mould, camped with
Death where the dead men lie.

---

Barcroft Boake (1866–92) is succinctly described by the
*Australian Dictionary of Biography* as 'physically tough,
emotionally sensitive, temperamentally unstable, financially
inept'. He suffered what today is called bipolar disorder and
hung himself with his stockwhip in Sydney scrubland at
the comparatively young age of 26. Much of his reputation
rests on this poem, which was first printed in *The Bulletin*
on 19 December 1891 under the pseudonym 'Surcingle'.

# JACK'S LAST MUSTER

### *Barcroft Boake*

The first flush of grey light, the herald of daylight,
Is dimly outlining the musterers' camp,
Where over the sleeping the stealthily creeping
Breath of the morning lies chilly and damp,

As, blankets forsaking, 'twixt sleeping and waking,
The black-boys turn out to the manager's call –
Whose order, of course, is, "Be after the horses,
And take all sorts of care you unhobble them all!"

Then, each with a bridle (provokingly idle),
They saunter away his commands to fulfil,
Where, cheerily chiming, the musical rhyming
From equine bell-ringers comes over the hill.

But now the dull dawning gives place to the morning:
The sun, springing up in a glorious flood
Of golden-shot fire, mounts higher and higher,
Till the crests of the sandhills are stained with his blood.

Now the hobble-chains' jingling, with thud of hoofs mingling,
Though distant, sound near – the cool air is so still –
As, urged by their whooping, the horses come trooping
In front of the boys round the point of the hill.

What searching and rushing for bridles and brushing
Of saddle marks, tight'ning of breastplate and girth!
And what a strange jumble of laughter and grumble –
Some comrade's misfortune the subject of mirth.

I recollect well how that morning Jack Bell
Had an argument over the age of a mare,
That C O B gray one, the dam of that bay one
Which storekeeper Brown calls the Young Lady Clare;

How Tomboy and Vanity caused much profanity,
Scamp'ring away with their tails in the air,
Till after a chase at a deuce of a pace,
They ran back in the mob and we collared them there.

Then the laugh and the banter, as gaily we canter,
With a pause for the nags at a miniature lake,
Where the yellowtop catches the sunlight in patches,
And lies like a mirror of gold in our wake.

O, the rush and the rattle of fast-fleeing cattle,
Whose hoofs beat a mad rataplan on the earth!
Their hot-headed flight in! Who would not delight in
The gallop that seems to hold all life is worth?

And over the rolling plains slowly patrolling
To the sound of the cattle's monotonous tramp,
Till we hear the sharp pealing of stockwhips, revealing
The fact that our comrades have put on the camp.

From the spot where they're drafting the wind rises, wafting
The dust till it hides man and beast from our gaze,
Till, suddenly lifting and easterly drifting,
We catch a short glimpse of the scene through the haze –

A blending and blurring of swiftly recurring
Colour and movement, that pass on their way;
An intricate weaving of sights and sounds, leaving
An eager desire to take part in the fray;

A dusty procession, in circling succession,
Of bullocks that bellow in impotent rage;
A bright panorama, a soul-stirring drama –
The sky for its background, the earth for its stage.

How well I remember that twelfth of November,
When Jack and his little mare, Vanity, fell!
On the Diamantina there never was seen a
Pair who could cut out a beast half as well.

And yet in one second Death's finger had beckoned,
And horse and bold rider had answered the call
Brooking no hesitation, without preparation,
That sooner or later must come to us all.

Thrice a big curly-horned Cobb bullock had scorned
To meekly acknowledge the ruling of Fate;
Thrice Jack with a clout of his whip cut him out,
But each time the beast galloped back to his mate.

Once more, he came blund'ring along, with Jack thund'ring
Beside him, his spurs in poor Vanity's flanks,
When, from some cause or other forsaking its mother,
A little white calf trotted out from the ranks.

'Twas useless, I knew it; yet I turned to pursue it:
At the same time I gave a loud warning to Jack:
It was all unavailing: I saw him come sailing
Along as the weaner ran into his track.

Little Vanity tried to turn off on one side,
Then altered her mind and attempted to leap . . .
The pace was too fast: that jump was her last;
For she and her rider fell all in a heap.

I was quickly down kneeling beside him, and feeling
With tremulous hand for the throb of his heart.
"The mare – is she dead?" were the first words he said,
As he suddenly opened his eyes with a start.

He spoke to the creature – his hand could just reach her –
Gently caressing her lean Arab head;
She acknowledged his praising with eyes quickly glazing . . .
A whinny . . . a struggle . . . and there she lay dead!

I sat there and nursed his head, for we durst
Not remove him: we knew where he fell he would die.
As I watched his life flicker, his breath growing thicker,
I'd have given the world to be able to cry.

Rough-voiced, sunburnt men, far away beyond ken
Of civilisation, our comrades, stood nigh –
All true-hearted mourners, and sadly forlorn as
He gave them a handshake and bade them goodbye.

In my loving embrace there he finished life's race,
And nobly and gamely that long course was run;
Though a man and a sinner he weighed out a winner,
And God, the Great Judge, will declare he has won.

---

The Diamantina River is in western Queensland.

C O B = a cattle brand for Cobb & Co., the pastoral arm of
the famous coaching enterprise
*dam* = a female horse
*yellowtop* = common name for the yellow-flowered pannick grass
*rataplan* = drumbeat

# HARVEST TIME

### Charles Souter

When the cranky German waggon,
With its ten or fifteen bag on
Comes a-jerkin' and a-joltin' down the dusty, limestone street,
And the "Norther's" blowin' blindin',
And the rollers are a-grindin',
And the agent jabs his sampler thro' the sackin' to the wheat,
Let 'em slide along the plank! slide along! slide along!
Sixty bushels for the Bank; slide along!

When your back is fairly breakin'
And your very fingers shakin'
With the heavin', heavin', heavin', in the blarsted, blazin' sun;
And the agent finds the spots out
And takes all his sample lots out
Where it's rusty, pinched, or smutty – knockin' off five pound a ton;
Sling 'em over with a jerk! slide along! slide along!

Sixty days of wasted work! slide along!
Sixty days a-ploughin' mallee
In the God-forgotten valley
Of the creepin', crawlin' Murray, with the dingoes for your mates!
Sow and harrow, roll and reap it,
But you get no show to keep it,
For it's "Boom and bust yer biler" when the cocky speculates!
Let the bankers take the lot: slide along! slide along!
Farmin' mallee's bloomin' rot – slide along!

. . . over

Charles H. Souter (1864–1944), who wrote as 'Nil' or 'Dr Nil' and contributed regularly to *The Bulletin*, is not known as widely as many of his contemporaries, nor as much as he deserves. Born in Scotland, his early life was unsettled, spent partly at sea and partly in the Australian outback. A qualified doctor, he finally set up practices in a number of South Australian country towns.

The moment of truth for the wheat farmer was when he trucked his harvest to town. Here the local agent would jab a small metal scoop into the sides of selected sacks to sample the grain's quality. This might reveal traces of the fungal diseases, rust and smut, and so lower the price the farmer had hoped for. Most of the income was owed to the bank anyhow.

*bust yer biler* = 'bust your boiler', meaning to over-exert yourself

# PETER SIMSON'S FARM

## *Edward Dyson*

Simson settled in the timber when his arm was strong and true
And his form was straight and limber; and he wrought the long day through
In a struggle, single-handed, and the trees fell slowly back,
Twenty thousand giants banded 'gainst a solitary Jack.

Through the fiercest days of summer you might hear his keen axe ring
And re-echo in the ranges, hear his twanging crosscut sing;
Then the great gums swayed and whispered, and the birds were skyward blown,
As the circling hills saluted o'er a bush king overthrown.

Clearing, grubbing, in the gloaming, strong in faith the man descried
Heifers sleek and horses roaming in his paddocks green and wide,
Heard a myriad corn-blades rustle in the breeze's soft caress,
And in every thew and muscle felt a joyous mightiness.

So he felled the stubborn forest, hacked and hewed with tireless might,
And a conqueror's peace went with him to his fern-strewn bunk at night:
Forth he strode next morn, delighting in the duty to be done,
Whistling shrilly to the magpies trilling carols to the sun.

Back the clustered scrub was driven, and the sun fell on the lands,
And the mighty stumps were riven 'tween his bare, brown, corded hands.
One time flooded, sometimes parching, still he did the work of ten,
And his dog-leg fence went marching up the hills and down again.

By the stony creek, whose tiny streams slid o'er the sunken bowls
To their secret, silent meetings in the shaded water-holes,
Soon a garden flourished bravely, gemmed with flowers, and cool and green,
While about the hut a busy little wife was always seen.

Came a day at length when, gazing down the paddock from his door,
Simson saw his horses grazing where the bush was long before,
And he heard the joyous prattle of his children on the rocks,
And the lowing of the cattle, and the crowing of the cocks.

There was butter for the market, there was fruit upon the trees,
There were eggs, potatoes, bacon, and a tidy lot of cheese;
Still the struggle was not ended with the timber and the scrub,
For the mortgage is the toughest stump the settler has to grub.

But the boys grew big and bolder – one, a sturdy, brown-faced lad,
With his axe upon his shoulder, loved to go to work 'like dad',
And another in the saddle took a bush-bred native's pride,
And he boasted he could straddle any nag his dad could ride.

Though the work went on and prospered there was still hard work to do;
There were floods, and droughts, and bush fires, and a touch of pleuro, too;
But they laboured, and the future held no prospect to alarm –
All the settlers said: 'They're stickers up at Peter Simson's farm.'

One fine evening Pete was resting in the hush of coming night,
When his boys came in from nesting with a clamorous delight;
Each displayed a tiny rabbit, and the farmer eyed them o'er,
Then he stamped – it was his habit – and he smote his knee and swore.

Two years later Simson's paddock showed dust-coloured, almost bare,
And too lean for hope of profit were the cows that pastured there,
And the man looked ten years older. Like the tracks about the place
Made by half a million rabbits, were the lines on Simson's face.

As he fought the bush when younger, Simson stripped and fought again,
Fought the devastating hunger of the plague with might and main,
Neither moping nor despairing, hoping still that times would mend,
Stubborn browed and sternly facing all the trouble Fate could send.

One poor chicken to the acre Simson's land will carry now.
Starved, the locusts have departed; rust is thick upon the plough;
It is vain to think of cattle, or to try to raise a crop,
For the farmer has gone under, and the rabbits are on top.

So the strong, true man who wrested from the bush a homestead fair,
By the rabbits has been bested; yet he does not know despair –
Though begirt with desolation, though in trouble and in debt,
Though his foes pass numeration, Peter Simson's fighting yet!

He is old too soon and failing, but he's game to start anew,
And he tells his hopeless neighbours 'what the Gov'mint's goin' to do'.
Both his girls are in the city, seeking places with the rest,
And his boys are tracking fortune in the melancholy West.

---

Edward Dyson (1865–1931) was one of three notably creative
brothers – the youngest, Will, became an internationally
acclaimed cartoonist and was married to Norman Lindsay's

sister, Ruby. Edward Dyson began his working life in mining, but ultimately became a full-time journalist and best known as a short-story writer, particularly for 'The Golden Shanty'. His verse collection, *Rhymes From the Mines*, was first published in 1896 and included this poem.

*pleuro* = pleuro-pneumonia

# HOW McDOUGAL
# TOPPED THE SCORE

### *Thomas E. Spencer*

A peaceful spot is Piper's Flat. The folk that live around,
They keep themselves by keeping sheep and turning up the ground.
But the climate is erratic, and the consequences are
The struggle with the elements is everlasting war.
We plough, and sow, and harrow – then sit down and pray for rain;
And then we all get flooded out and have to start again.
But the folk are now rejoicing as they ne'er rejoiced before,
For we've played Molongo cricket and McDougal topped the score!

Molongo had a head on it, and challenged us to play
A single-innings match for lunch – the losing team to pay.
We were not great guns at cricket, but we couldn't well say No,
So we all began to practise, and we let the reaping go.
We scoured the Flat for ten miles round to muster up our men,
But when the list was totalled we could only number ten.
Then up spoke big Tim Brady, he was always slow to speak,
And he said – "What price McDougal, who lives down at Cooper's Creek?"

So we sent for old McDougal, and he stated in reply
That "He'd never played at cricket, but he'd half a mind to try.
He couldn't come to practice – he was getting in his hay –
But he guessed he'd show the beggars from Molongo how to play."
Now, McDougal was a Scotchman, and a canny one at that,
So he started in to practise with a paling for a bat.

He got Mrs. Mac. to bowl to him, but she couldn't run at all,
So he trained his sheep dog, Pincher, how to scout and fetch the ball.

Now, Pincher was no puppy; he was old, and worn, and grey;
But he understood McDougal, and – accustomed to obey –
When McDougal cried out "Fetch it!" he would fetch it in a trice;
But until the word was "Drop it!" he would grip it like a vice.
And each succeeding night they played until the light grew dim;
Sometimes McDougal struck the ball – sometimes the ball struck *him*!
Each time he struck, the ball would plough a furrow in the ground,
And when he missed, the impetus would turn him three times round.

The fatal day at length arrived – the day that was to see
Molongo bite the dust, or Piper's Flat knocked up a tree!
Molongo's captain won the toss, and sent his men to bat,
And they gave some leather-hunting to the men of Piper's Flat.
When the ball sped where McDougal stood, firm planted in his track,
He shut his eyes, and turned him round, and stopped it with his *back*!
The highest score was twenty-two, the total sixty-six,
When Brady sent a yorker down that scattered Johnson's sticks.

Then Piper's Flat went in to bat, for glory and renown,
But, like the grass before the scythe, our wickets tumbled down.
"Nine wickets down for seventeen, with fifty more to win!"
Our captain heaved a sigh – and sent McDougal in.
"Ten pounds to one you'll lose it!" cried a barracker from town;
But McDougal said "I'll tak' it, mon!" and planked the money down.
Then he girded up his moleskins in a self-reliant style,
Threw off his hat and boots, and faced the bowler with a smile.

He held the bat the wrong side out, and Johnson with a grin,
Stepped lightly to the bowling crease, and sent a "wobbler" in;
McDougal spooned it softly back, and Johnson waited there,
But McDougal, crying *Fetch it!* started running like a hare.
Molongo shouted "Victory! He's out as sure as eggs."
When Pincher started through the crowd, and ran through Johnson's legs.
He seized the ball like lightning; then he ran behind a log,
And McDougal kept on running, while Molongo chased the dog.

They chased him up, they chased him down, they chased him round, and then
He darted through the slip-rail as the scorer shouted "Ten!"
McDougal puffed; Molongo swore; excitement was intense;
As the scorer marked down "Twenty", Pincher cleared a barbed-wire fence.
"Let us head him!" shrieked Molongo, "Brain the mongrel with a bat!"
"Run it out! Good old McDougal!" yelled the men from Piper's Flat.
And McDougal kept on jogging, and then Pincher doubled back,
And the scorer counted *"Forty"* as they raced across the track.

McDougal's legs were going fast, Molongo's breath was gone –
But still Molongo chased the dog – McDougal struggled on.
When the scorer shouted *"Fifty!"*, then they knew the chase would cease;
And McDougal gasped out "Drop it!" as *he* dropped within his crease.
Then Pincher dropped the ball, and, as instinctively he knew
Discretion was the wiser plan, he disappeared from view.
And as Molongo's beaten men exhausted lay around,
We raised McDougal shoulder high and bore him from the ground.

We bore him to McGinniss's, where lunch was ready laid,
And filled him up with whisky-punch, for which Molongo paid.

We drank his health in bumpers, and we cheered him three times three,
And when Molongo got its breath, Molongo joined the spree.
And the critics say they never saw a cricket match like that,
When McDougal broke the record in the game at Piper's Flat.
And the folk are jubilating as they never did before;
For we played Molongo cricket – and *McDougal topped the score!*

Thomas E. Spencer migrated from London to Sydney in 1875
and set up as a building contractor, working, *inter alia*, on
the construction of Goulburn gaol. He began contributing
prose and verse to *The Bulletin* in 1891. Archibald welcomed
him with this observation: 'Your verses blew into the office
like a whiff from the bush. It was a pleasure to read some
lines which did not contain wattle and dead men.'

# HOW WE DROVE THE TROTTER

### W.T. *Goodge*

Oh, he was a handsome trotter, and he couldn't be completer,
He had such a splendid action and he trotted to this metre,
Such a pace and such a courage, such a record-killing power,
That he did his mile in two-fifteen, his twenty in the hour.
When he trotted on the Bathurst road the pace it was a panter,
But he broke the poet's rhythm when he broke out in a canter –

As we were remarking the pace was a panter,
But just as we liked it he broke in a canter,
And rattled along with a motion terrific,
And scattered the sparks with a freedom prolific;
He tugged at the bit and he jerked at the bridle,
We pulled like a demon, the effort was idle,
The bit in his teeth and the rein in the crupper,
We didn't much care to get home to our supper.

> Then we went
> Like the wind,
> And our hands
> They were skinned,
> And we thought
> With a dread

To go over his head,
And we tugged
And we strove,
Couldn't say
That we drove
Till we found
It had stopped
And the gallop was dropped!

Then he dropped into a trot again as steady as a pacer,
And we thought we had a dandy that was sure to make a racer
That would rival all the Yankees and was bound to beat the British,
Not a bit of vice about him though he was a trifle skittish;
Past the buggies and the sulkies on the road we went a-flying,
For the pace it was a clinker, and they had no chance of trying,
But for fear he'd start a canter we were going to stop his caper
When he bolted like a bullet at a flying piece of paper –

Helter skelter,
What a pelter!
Such a pace to win a welter!
    Rush,
    Race,
    Tear!
  Flying through the air!
Wind a-humming,
Fears benumbing,
Here's another trap a-coming!
    Shouts!

Bash!
Crash!
Moses, what a smash!

---

William Thomas (W.T.) Goodge was born in London in 1862 and arrived in Sydney in 1882. He roamed around outback New South Wales for twelve years before settling on life as a journalist. For a time he was editor of the Orange *Leader* while contributing to *The Bulletin*. For the nine years prior to his death he wrote a weekly piece for the Sydney *Truth* concerning the doings of an imaginary drinking group, the Gimcrack Club. During his lifetime he published only one collection of poems: *Hits! Skits! and Jingles!* in 1899.

Goodge introduced a new exuberance to Australian versifying and a great awareness of the idiosyncrasies of Australian idiom. In many ways he was an important precursor to the humorous achievement of C.J. Dennis. Although under-rated by posterity, he was judged by Norman Lindsay as one of Australia's best writers of light verse. He died in 1909.

This poem and the many that follow later are typical examples of his great whimsicality that is now attracting new admirers.

# A SNAKE YARN

**W.T. Goodge**

"You talk of snakes," said Jack the Rat,
   "But blow me, one hot summer,
I seen a thing that knocked me flat –
Fourteen foot long or more than that,
   It was a reg'lar hummer!
Lay right along a sort of bog,
     Just like a log!

"The ugly thing was lyin' there
   And not a sign o' movin',
Give any man a nasty scare;
Seen nothin' like it anywhere
   Since I first started drovin'.
And yet it didn't scare my dog.
     *Looked* like a log!

"I had to cross that bog, yer see,
   And bluey I was humpin';
But wonderin' what that thing could be
A-lyin' there in front o' me
   I didn't feel like jumpin'.
Yet, though I shivered like a frog,
     It *seemed* a log!

"I takes a leap and lands right on
   The back of that there whopper!"
He stopped. We waited. Then Big Mac
Remarked: "Well, then, what happened, Jack?"
   "Not much," said Jack, and drained his grog.
      "It was a *log*!"

# THE GREAT
# *BULLETIN DEBATE*

Although Paterson admired Lawson greatly and at times attempted to assist him in the practical conduct of his life, these two giants of the early days of *The Bulletin* held diametrically different visions of rural Australia.

In July 1892, Lawson published his poem 'Borderland' (later retitled 'Up the Country'). He claimed to have returned to Sydney after seeking the enchanting land depicted by nameless 'Southern poets'. But he had discovered instead a dismal place, of barren desolation and treacherous tracks. A fortnight later The Banjo leapt in with his 'In Defence of the Bush', and it was on for young and old. Other writers, such as Edward Dyson, contributed to the ensuing controversy.

It appears that this began as a set-up, to line the pockets of the young Lawson and Paterson. As the latter remembered it in the tranquillity of 1939:

*Henry Lawson was a man of remarkable insight in some things and of extraordinary simplicity in others. We were both looking for the same reef, if you get what I mean; but I had done my prospecting on horseback with my meals cooked for me, while*

*Lawson has done his prospecting on foot and had had to cook for himself. Nobody realised this better than Lawson; and one day he suggested that we should write against each other, he putting the bush from his point of view, and I putting it from mine. "We ought to do pretty well out of it," he said, "we ought to be able to get in three or four sets of verses before they stop us."*

*This suited me all right, for we were working on space, and the pay was very small . . . so we slam-banged away at each other for weeks and weeks; not until they stopped us, but until we ran out of material . . .*

# BORDERLAND

### Henry Lawson

I am back from up the country – very sorry that I went –
Seeking for the Southern poets' land whereon to pitch my tent;
I have lost a lot of idols, which were broken on the track,
Burnt a lot of fancy verses, and I'm glad that I am back.
Further out may be the pleasant scenes of which our poets boast,
But I think the country's rather more inviting round the coast.
Anyway, I'll stay at present at a boarding-house in town,
Drinking beer and lemon-squashes, taking baths and cooling down.

'Sunny plains'! Great Scott! – those burning wastes of barren soil and sand
With their everlasting fences stretching out across the land!
Desolation where the crow is! Desert where the eagle flies,
Paddocks where the luny bullock starts and stares with reddened eyes;
Where, in clouds of dust enveloped, roasted bullock-drivers creep
Slowly past the sun-dried shepherd dragged behind his crawling sheep.
Stunted peak of granite gleaming, glaring like a molten mass
Turned from some infernal furnace on a plain devoid of grass.

Miles and miles of thirsty gutters – strings of muddy water-holes
In the place of 'shining rivers' – 'walled by cliffs and forest boles.'
Barren ridges, gullies, ridges! where the ever-madd'ning flies –
Fiercer than the plagues of Egypt – swarm about your blighted eyes!
Bush! where there is no horizon! where the buried bushman sees
Nothing – Nothing! but the sameness of the ragged, stunted trees!

Lonely hut where drought's eternal, suffocating atmosphere
Where the God-forgotten hatter dreams of city life and beer.

Treacherous tracks that trap the stranger, endless roads that gleam and glare,
Dark and evil-looking gullies, hiding secrets here and there!
Dull dumb flats and stony rises, where the toiling bullocks bake,
And the sinister 'gohanna', and the lizard, and the snake.
Land of day and night – no morning freshness, and no afternoon,
When the great white sun in rising bringeth summer heat in June.
Dismal country for the exile, when the shades begin to fall
From the sad heart-breaking sunset, to the new-chum worst of all.

Dreary land in rainy weather, with the endless clouds that drift
O'er the bushman like a blanket that the Lord will never lift –
Dismal land when it is raining – growl of floods, and, oh! the woosh
Of the rain and wind together on the dark bed of the bush –
Ghastly fires in lonely humpies where the granite rocks are piled
In the rain-swept wildernesses that are wildest of the wild.

Land where gaunt and haggard women live alone and work like men,
Till their husbands, gone a-droving, will return to them again:
Homes of men! if home had ever such a God-forgotten place,
Where the wild selector's children fly before a stranger's face.
Home of tragedy applauded by the dingoes' dismal yell,
Heaven of the shanty-keeper – fitting fiend for such a hell –
And the wallaroos and wombats, and, of course, the curlew's call –
And the lone sundowner tramping ever onward through it all!

I am back from up the country, up the country where I went
Seeking for the Southern poets' land whereon to pitch my tent;
I have shattered many idols out along the dusty track,
Burnt a lot of fancy verses – and I'm glad that I am back.
I believe the Southern poets' dream will not be realised
Till the plains are irrigated and the land is humanised.
I intend to stay at present, as I said before, in town
Drinking beer and lemon-squashes, taking baths and cooling down.

*The Bulletin*, 9 July 1892

---

*luny* = old spelling of 'loony', meaning lunatic

# IN DEFENCE OF THE BUSH

### A.B. *Paterson*

So you're back from up the country, Mister Lawson, where you went,
And you're cursing all the business in a bitter discontent;
Well, we grieve to disappoint you, and it makes us sad to hear
That it wasn't cool and shady – and there wasn't plenty beer,
And the loony bullock snorted when you first came into view;
Well, you know it's not so often that he sees a swell like you;
And the roads were hot and dusty, and the plains were burnt and brown,
And no doubt you're better suited drinking lemon-squash in town.
Yet, perchance, if you should journey down the very track you went
In a month or two at furthest you would wonder what it meant,
Where the sunbaked earth was gasping like a creature in its pain
You would find the grasses waving like a field of summer grain,
And the miles of thirsty gutters blocked with sand and choked with mud,
You would find them mighty rivers with a turbid, sweeping flood;
For the rain and drought and sunshine make no changes in the street,
In the sullen line of buildings and the ceaseless tramp of feet;
But the bush hath moods and changes, as the seasons rise and fall,
And the men who know the bush-land – they are loyal through it all.

　　　* * *

But you found the bush was dismal and a land of no delight,
Did you chance to hear a chorus in the shearers' huts at night?
Did they 'rise up, William Riley' by the camp-fire's cheery blaze?

Did they rise him as we rose him in the good old droving days?
And the women of the homesteads and the men you chanced to meet –
Were their faces sour and saddened like the 'faces in the street',
And the 'shy selector children' – were they better now or worse
Than the little city urchins who would greet you with a curse?
Is not such a life much better than the squalid street and square
Where the fallen women flaunt it in the fierce electric glare,
Where the sempstress plies her sewing till her eyes are sore and red
In a filthy, dirty attic toiling on for daily bread?
Did you hear no sweeter voices in the music of the bush
Than the roar of trams and 'buses, and the war-whoop of 'the push'?
Did the magpies rouse your slumbers with their carol sweet and strange?
Did you hear the silver chiming of the bell-birds on the range?
But, perchance, the wild birds' music by your senses was despised,
For you say you'll stay in townships till the bush is civilised.
Would you make it a tea-garden and on Sundays have a band
Where the 'blokes' might take their 'donahs', with a 'public' close at hand?
You had better stick to Sydney and make merry with the 'push',
For the bush will never suit you, and you'll never suit the bush.

*The Bulletin*, 23 July 1892

---

rise up, William Riley = The Irish folk song usually called 'The
Trial of Willy Reilly' was popular in the colonies; it began:
'O rise up, Willy Reilly, & come away with me, / For I do mean
to go with you & leave this countrie'
*sempstress* = variant spelling of seamstress

# THE FACT OF THE MATTER

## *Edward Dyson*

I'm wonderin' why those fellers who go buildin' chipper ditties,
'Bout the rosy times out drovin', an' the dust an' death of cities,
Don't sling the bloomin' office, strike some drover for a billet,
And soak up all the glory that comes handy while they fill it.
P'r'aps it's fun to travel cattle or to picnic with merinos,
But the drover don't catch on, sir, not much high-class rapture he knows.
As for sleepin' on the plains there in the shadder of the spear-grass,
That's liked best by the Juggins with a spring-bed an' a pier-glass.
An' the camp-fire, an' the freedom, and the blanky constellations,
The 'possum-rug an' billy, an' the togs an' stale ole rations –
It's strange they're only raved about by coves that dress up pretty,
An' sport a wife, an' live on slap-up tucker in the city.
I've tickled beef in my time clear from Clarke to Riverina,
An' shifted sheep all round the shop, but blow me if I've seen a
Single blanky hand who didn't buck at pleasures of this kidney,
And wouldn't trade his blisses for a flutter down in Sydney.
Night-watches are delightful when the stars are really splendid
To the chap who's fresh upon the job, but, you bet, his rapture's ended
When the rain comes down in sluice-heads, or the cuttin' hailstones pelter,
An' the sheep drift off before the wind, an' the horses strike for shelter.
Don't take me for a howler, but I find it come annoyin'
To hear these fellers rave about the pleasures we're enjoyin',
When p'r'aps we've nothin' better than some fluky water handy,
An' they're right on all the lickers – rum, an' plenty beer an' brandy.

The town is dusty, may be, but it isn't worth the curses
'Side the dust a feller swallers an' the blinded thirst he nurses
When he's on the hard macadam, where the jumbucks cannot browse, an'
The wind is in his whiskers, an' he follers twenty thousan'.
This drovin' on the plain, too, it's all O.K. when the weather
Isn't hot enough to curl the soles right off your upper leather,
Or so cold that when the mornin' wind comes hissin' through the grasses
You can feel it cut your eyelids like a whip-lash as it passes.
Then there's bull-ants in the blankets, an' a lame horse, an' muskeeters,
An' a D.T. boss like Halligan, or one like Humpy Peters,
Who is mean about the tucker, an' can curse from start to sundown,
An' can fight like fifty devils, an' whose growler's never run down.
Yes, I wonder why the fellers what go building chipper ditties
'Bout the rosy times out drovin' an' the dust an' death of cities,
Don't sling the bloomin' office, strike ole Peters for a billet,
An' soak up all the glory that comes handy while they fill it.

*The Bulletin*, 30 July 1892

---

shadder = shadow
pier-glass = a long mirror
fluky water = water from an unreliable source
macadam = a road of broken stones
musketeers = an idiomatic rendering of mosquitoes
D.T. = delirium tremens, the tragic and then prevalent
manifestation of advanced alcoholism

# IN ANSWER TO BANJO, AND OTHERWISE

### Henry Lawson

It was pleasant up the country, Mr. Banjo, where you went,
For you sought the greener patches and you travelled like a gent.,
And you curse the trams and 'busses and the turmoil and the "push",
Tho' you know the "squalid city" needn't keep you from the bush;
But we lately heard you singing of the "plains where shade is not",
And you mentioned it was dusty – "all is dry and all is hot".

True, the bush "hath moods and changes," and the bushman hath 'em, too –
For he's not a poet's dummy – he's a man, the same as you;
But his back is growing rounder – slaving for the "absentee" –
And his toiling wife is thinner than a country wife should be,
For we noticed that the faces of the folks we chanced to meet
Should have made a stronger contrast to the faces in the street;
And, in short, we think the bushman's being driven to the wall,
But it's doubtful if his spirit will be "*loyal* thro' it all."

Tho' the bush has been romantic and it's nice to sing about,
There's a lot of patriotism that the land could do without –
Sort of BRITISH WORKMEN nonsense that shall perish in the scorn
Of the drover who is driven and the shearer who is shorn –
Of the struggling western farmers who have little time for rest,
And are ruin'd on selections in the squatter-ridden west –

Droving songs are very pretty, but they merit little thanks
From the people of country which is ridden by the Banks.

And the "rise and fall of seasons" suits the rise and fall of rhyme,
But we know that western seasons do not run on "schedule time";
For the drought will go on drying while there's anything to dry,
Then it rains until you'd fancy it would bleach the "sunny sky" –
Then it pelters out of reason, for the downpour day and night
Nearly sweeps the population to the Great Australian Bight,
It is up in Northern Queensland that the "seasons" do their best,
But its doubtful if you ever saw a season in the west,
There are years without an autumn or a winter or a spring,
There are broiling Junes – and summers when it rains like anything.

In the bush my ears were opened to the singing of the bird,
But the "carol of the magpie" was a thing I never heard.
Once the beggar roused my slumbers in a shanty, it is true,
But I only heard him asking, "Who the blanky blank are you?"
And the bell-bird in the ranges – but his "silver chime" is harsh
When it's heard beside the solo of the curlew in the marsh.

Yes, I heard the shearers singing "William Riley" out of tune
(Saw 'em fighting round a shanty on a Sunday afternoon),
But the bushman isn't always "trapping bunnies in the night",
Nor is he ever riding when "the morn is fresh and bright",
And he isn't always singing in the humpies on the run –
And the camp-fire's "cheery blazes" are a trifle overdone;
We have grumbled with the bushmen round the fire on rainy days,
When the smoke would blind a bullock and there wasn't any blaze,

Save the blazes of our language, for we cursed the fire in turn
Till the atmosphere was heated and the wood began to burn.
Then we had to wring our blueys which were rotting in the swags,
And we saw the sugar leaking thro' the bottoms of the bags,
And we couldn't raise a "chorus", for the toothache and the cramp,
While we spent the hours of darkness draining puddles round the camp.

Would you like to change with Clancy – go a-droving? tell us true,
For we rather think that Clancy would be glad to change with you,
And be something in the city; but 'twould give your muse a shock
To be losing time and money thro' the foot-rot in the flock,
And you wouldn't mind the beauties underneath the starry dome
If you had a wife and children and a lot of bills at home.

Did you ever guard the cattle when the night was inky-black,
And it rained, and icy water trickled gently down your back
Till your saddle-weary backbone fell a-aching to the roots
And you almost felt the croaking of the bull-frog in your boots –
Sit and shiver in the saddle, curse the restless stock and cough
Till a squatter's irate dummy cantered up to warn you off?
Did you fight the drought and "pleuro" when the "seasons" were asleep –
Falling she-oaks all the morning for a flock of starving sheep;
Drinking mud instead of water – climbing trees and lopping boughs
For the broken-hearted bullocks and the dry and dusty cows?

Do you think the bush was better in the "good old droving days",
When the squatter ruled supremely as the king of western ways,
When you got a slip of paper for the little you could earn,
But were forced to take provisions from the station in return –

When you couldn't keep a chicken at your humpy on the run,
For the squatter wouldn't let you – and your work was never done:
When you had to leave the missus in a lonely hut forlorn
While you "rose up Willy Riley", in the days ere you were born?

Ah! we read about the drovers and the shearers and the like
Till we wonder why such happy and romantic fellows "strike".
Don't you fancy that the poets better give the bush a rest
Ere they raise a just rebellion in the over-written West?
Where the simple-minded bushman get a meal and bed and rum
Just by riding round reporting phantom flocks that never come;
Where the scalper – never troubled by the "war-whoop of the push" –
Has a quiet little billet – breeding rabbits in the bush;
Where the idle shanty-keeper never fails to make a "draw",
And the dummy gets his tucker thro' provisions in the law;
Where the labour-agitator – when the shearers rise in might
Makes his money sacrificing all his substance for the right;
Where the squatter makes his fortune, and the seasons "rise" and "fall",
And the poor and honest bushman has to suffer for it all,
Where the drovers and the shearers and the bushmen and the rest
Never reach the Eldorado of the poets of the West.

And you think the bush is purer and that life is better there,
But it doesn't seem to pay you like the "squalid street and square",
Pray inform us, "Mr. Banjo", where you read, in prose or verse,
Of the awful "city urchin" who would greet you with a curse.
There are golden hearts in gutters, tho' their owners lack the fat,
And we'll back a teamster's offspring to outswear a city brat;
Do you think we're never jolly where the trams and 'busses rage?

Did you hear the "gods" in chorus when "Ri-tooral" held the stage?
Did you catch a ring of sorrow in the city urchin's voice
When he yelled for "Billy Elton," when he thumped the floor for Royce?
Do the bushmen, down on pleasure, miss the everlasting stars
When they drink and flirt and so on in the glow of private bars?
What care you if fallen women "flaunt"? God help 'em – let 'em flaunt,
And the seamstress seems to haunt you – to what purpose does she haunt?
You've a down on "trams and busses", or the "roar" of 'em, you said,
And the "filthy, dirty attic", where you never toiled for bread.
(And about that self-same attic, tell us, Banjo, where you've been?
For the struggling needlewoman mostly keeps her attic clean.)
But you'll find it very jolly with the cuff-and-collar push,
And the city seems to suit you, while you rave about the bush.


P.S. –


You'll admit that "up-the-country", more especially in drought,
Isn't quite the Eldorado that the poets rave about,
Yet at times we long to gallop where the reckless bushman rides
In the wake of startled brumbies that are flying for their hides;
Long to feel the saddle tremble once again between our knees
And to hear the stockwhips rattle just like rifles in the trees!
Long to feel the bridle-leather tugging strongly in the hand
And to feel once more a little like a "native of the land".
And the ring of bitter feeling in the jingling of our rhymes
Isn't suited to the country nor the spirit of the times.
Let's us go together droving and returning, if we live,
Try to understand each other while we liquor up the "div".

*The Bulletin*, 6 August 1892

*dummy* = an agent of the squatter

*scalpers* = rabbit-exterminators, paid per 'scalp'

*shanty* = generally, a rough hut; but also rudimentary and unlicensed bush pubs, run by 'shanty-keepers'

*the gods* = the cheapest seats in the theatre – high up and far from the stage

'*Ri-tooral*' = probably a reference to the song these days known as *Botany Bay*

*liquor up the div* = to drink the rural proceeds

# IN ANSWER TO VARIOUS BARDS

## A.B. Paterson

Well, I've waited mighty patient while they all came rolling in,
Mister Lawson, Mister Dyson, and the others of their kin,
With their dreadful, dismal stories of the Overlander's camp,
How his fire is always smoky, and his boots are always damp;
And they paint it so terrific it would fill one's soul with gloom,
But you know they're fond of writing about "corpses" and "the tomb".
So, before they curse the bushland they should let their fancy range,
And take something for their livers, and be cheerful for a change.

Now, for instance, Mr. Lawson – well, of course, we almost cried
At the sorrowful description how his "little 'Arvie" died,
And we lachrymosed in silence when "His Father's Mate" was slain;
Then he went and killed the father, and we had to weep again.
Ben Duggan and Jack Denver, too, he caused them to expire,
And he went and cooked the gander of Jack Dunn, of Nevertire;
And, no doubt, the bush is wretched if you judge it by the groan
Of the sad and soulful poet with a graveyard of his own.

And he spoke in terms prophetic of a revolution's heat,
When the world should hear the clamour of those people in the street;
But the shearer chaps who start it – why, he rounds on them in blame,
And he calls 'em "agitators" who are living on the game.
But I "over-write" the bushmen! Well, I own without a doubt
That I always see a hero in the "man from furthest out".

I could never contemplate him through an atmosphere of gloom,
And a bushman never struck me as a subject for "the tomb".

If it ain't all "golden sunshine" where the "wattle branches wave",
Well, it ain't all damp and dismal, and it ain't all "lonely grave".
And, of course, there's no denying that the bushman's life is rough,
But a man can easy stand it if he's built of sterling stuff;
Tho' it's seldom that the drover gets a bed of eider-down,
Yet the man who's born a bushman, he gets mighty sick of town,
For he's jotting down the figures, and he's adding up the bills
While his heart is simply aching for a sight of Southern hills.

Then he hears a wool-team passing with a rumble and a lurch,
And, although the work is pressing, yet it brings him off his perch.
For it stirs him like a message from his station friends afar
And he seems to sniff the ranges in the scent of wool and tar;
And it takes him back in fancy, half in laughter, half in tears,
To a sound of other voices and a thought of other years,
When the woolshed rang with bustle from the dawning of the day,
And the shear-blades were a-clicking to the cry of "Wool away!"

Then his face was somewhat browner, and his frame was firmer set –
And he feels his flabby muscles with a feeling of regret.
But the wool-team slowly passes, and his eyes go slowly back
To the dusty little table and the papers in the rack,
And his thoughts go to the terrace where his sickly children squall,
And he thinks there's something healthy in the bush-life after all.
But we'll go no more a-droving in the wind or in the sun,
For our fathers' hearts have failed us, and the droving days are done.

There's a nasty dash of danger where the long-horned bullock wheels,
And we like to live in comfort and to get our reg'lar meals.
For to hang around the township suits us better, you'll agree,
And a job at washing bottles is the job for such as we.
Let us herd into the cities, let us crush and crowd and push
Till we lose the love of roving, and we learn to hate the bush;
And we'll turn our aspirations to a city life and beer,
And we'll slip across to England – it's a nicer place than here;

For there's not much risk of hardship where all comforts are in store,
And the theatres are in plenty, and the pubs are more and more.
But that ends it, Mr. Lawson, and it's time to say good-bye,
We must agree to differ in all friendship, you and I;
So we'll work our own salvation with the stoutest hearts we may,
And if fortune only favours we will take the road some day,
And go droving down the river 'neath the sunshine and the stars,
And then return to Sydney and vermilionize the bars.

*The Bulletin*, 1 October 1892

---

'Arvie Aspinall's Alarm Clock' and 'His Father's Mate'
are two of Lawson's best-loved short stories; 'Jack Dunn
of Nevertire' and 'Ben Duggan' (in which Jack Denver
appears) are two of his poems.

# BANJO, OF THE OVERFLOW

### Francis Kenna

I had written him a letter, which I had for want of better
Knowledge given to a partner by the name of "Greenhide Jack" –
He was shearing when I met him, and I thought perhaps I'd let him
Know that I was "stiff", and, maybe, he would send a trifle back.

My request was not requited, for an answer came indited
On a sheet of scented paper, in an ink of fancy blue;
And the envelope, I fancy, had an "Esquire" to the Clancy,
And it simply read, "I'm busy; but I'll see what I can do!"

To the vision land I can go, and I often think of the "Banjo" –
Of the boy I used to shepherd in the not so long ago,
He was not the bushman's kidney, and among the crowd of Sydney
He'll be more at home than mooning on the dreary Overflow.

He has clients now to fee him, and has friends to come and see him,
He can ride from morn to evening in the padded hansom cars,
And he sees the beauties blending where the throngs are never ending,
And at night the wond'rous women in the everlasting bars.

I am tired of reading prattle of the sweetly-lowing cattle
Stringing out across the open with the bushmen riding free;
I am sick at heart of roving up and down the country droving,
And of alternating damper with the salt-junk and the tea.

And from sleeping in the water on the droving trips I've caught a
Lively dose of rheumatism in my back and in my knee,
And in spite of verse it's certain that the sky's a leaky curtain –
It may suit the "Banjo" nicely, but it never suited me.

And the bush is very pretty when you view it from the city,
But it loses all its beauty when you face it "on the pad";
And the wildernesses haunt you, and the plains extended daunt you,
Till at times you come to fancy life will drive you mad.

But I somehow often fancy that I'd rather not be Clancy,
That I'd like to be the "Banjo" where the people come and go
When instead of framing curses I'd be writing charming verses –
Tho' I scarcely think he'd swap me, "Banjo, of the Overflow".

---

Although this poem by Francis Kenna (1865–1932) is not
usually included among the so-called 'Bulletin Controversy'
poems, it deserves to be as well known. It appeared in
The Bulletin on 27 August 1892.


stiff = broke
salt-junk = a hardy salt meat, usually offered to sailors
the pad = the distance travelled by foot, especially by swaggies

# FEDERATION
# FLAG-WAVING

From its earliest issues, *The Bulletin* had championed the cause of republicanism, as had Henry Lawson, whose first published poem was 'Song of the Republic'. In the 1880s there seemed to have been a faint glimmer of hope that the six colonies would come together as a republic, which might even include New Zealand and Fiji. However, by the late 1890s Australia was moving relentlessly towards nationhood and on 1 January 1901 the Commonwealth of Australia, a federation of six states, was solemnly established after royal proclamation.

This was a time of nation building and rampant nationalism. Already two popular patriotic songs existed that might well have done service as the national anthem – 'Song of Australia' and 'Advance Australia Fair' – but predictably 'God Save The Queen' (in this case Queen Victoria, who actually only survived for a month after the birth of the new nation) was adopted as the song for formal occasions. The Battle of the Anthems was thus postponed until 1974, when Gough Whitlam announced, after a polling of 60,000 citizens in a face-off between these two and 'Waltzing Matilda', that 'Advance Australia Fair' was henceforth to be Australia's official anthem.

Side by side with the two great nineteenth-century patriotic songs, other poems were composed in the years before Federation to give joyous expression to the growing sense of national pride.

# THE SONG OF AUSTRALIA

*Caroline Carleton*

There is a land where summer skies
Are gleaming with a thousand dyes
And blend in witching harmonies;
  Where grassy knoll and forest height,
  Are flushing in the rosy light,
  And all above is azure bright –
    Australia! Australia! Australia!

There is a land where homesteads peep
From sunny plain and woodland steep
And love and joy bright vigils keep;
  Where voices glad of childish glee
  Are mingling with the melody
  Of nature's hidden minstrelsy –
    Australia! Australia! Australia!

There is a land where treasures shine
Deep in the dark unfathomed mine
For worshippers at Mammon's Shrine;
  Where gold lies hid! Where rubies gleam!
  And fabled wealth no more doth seem
  The idle fancy of a dream
    Australia! Australia! Australia!

There is a land where honey flows
Where laughing corn luxuriant grows;
Land of the myrtle and the rose;
  On hill and plain from clust'ring vine
  Is gushing out the purple wine,
  And cups are quaffed to thee and thine –
    Australia! Australia! Australia!

There is a land where, floating free,
From mountain top to girdling sea,
A proud flag waves exultingly,
  And Freedom's sons the banner bear,
  No shackled slave can breathe the air;
  Fairest of Britain's daughter fair –
    Australia! Australia! Australia!

---

In 1859 the progressive South Australian town of Gawler, through its local Institute, offered ten guineas for the best Patriotic Song. They received 96 entries from all over Australia. Ultimately, the six judges gave the prize unanimously to the English-born poet Caroline Carleton, who had arrived in South Australia with her husband and two children in 1839.

The town then offered another ten guineas for the best musical setting for this poem and that was awarded to Carl Linger.

Its first public performance was at the Oddfellows Hall, Gawler, on 12 December 1859, when it was sung by Miss Mary Ann Alien, accompanied by a quartet and the Brunswick Brass Band of eight performers under the personal baton of the composer.

'The Song of Australia' was its original title, although it is sometimes known as 'Song For Australia'.

The words reproduced here are as written by Caroline Carleton.

# ADVANCE AUSTRALIA FAIR

### *Peter Dodds McCormick*

Australia's sons let us rejoice,
For we are young and free;
We've golden soil and wealth for toil,
Our home is girt by sea;
Our land abounds in Nature's gifts
Of beauty rich and rare;
In hist'ry's page, let ev'ry stage
Advance Australia fair.
In joyful strains then let us sing,
Advance Australia fair.

When gallant Cook from Albion sailed,
To trace wide oceans o'er,
True British courage bore him on,
Til he landed on our shore.
Then here he raised Old England's flag,
The standard of the brave;
"With all her faults we love her still"
"Britannia rules the wave."
In joyful strains then let us sing
Advance Australia fair.

While other nations of the globe
Behold us from afar,
We'll rise to high renown and shine

Like our glorious southern star;
From England soil and Fatherland,
Scotia and Erin fair,
Let all combine with heart and hand
To advance Australia fair.
In joyful strains then let us sing
Advance Australia fair.

Should foreign foe e'er sight our coast,
Or dare a foot to land,
We'll rouse to arms like sires of yore,
To guard our native strand;
Britannia then shall surely know,
Though oceans roll between,
Her sons in fair Australia's land
Still keep their courage green.
In joyful strains then let us sing
Advance Australia fair.

---

'Advance Australia Fair' was composed by Scots-born
Peter Dodds McCormick and first performed at a Highland
Society function in Sydney on 30 November 1878. It quickly
gained popularity and an amended version was sung by a
choir of 10,000 at the inauguration of the Commonwealth
of Australia on 1 January 1901. In 1907 the Australian
Government awarded McCormick £100 for his composition.

McCormick later described the circumstances that inspired
him to write 'Advance Australia Fair': 'One night I attended
a great concert in the Exhibition Building, when all the

National Anthems of the world were to be sung by a large choir with band accompaniment. This was very nicely done, but I felt very aggravated that there was not one note for Australia. On the way home in a bus, I concocted the first verse of my song and when I got home I set it to music.'

'Advance Australia Fair' was proclaimed as the national anthem on 19 April 1984 by Governor-General Sir Ninian Stephen. It is used on all occasions except when the Royal Anthem or the Vice-Regal salute is used. The text here is that of the original version. Australia's current national anthem is a sanitised version of the above.

# MEN OF AUSTRALIA

### *Edward Dyson*

Men of all the lands Australian from the Gulf to Derwent River,
From the Heads of Sydney Harbour to the waters of the West,
There's a spirit loudly calling where the saplings dip and quiver,
Where the city crowds are thronging, and the range uplifts its crest!
Do ye feel the holy fervour of a new-born exultation?
For the task the Lord has set us is a trust of noblest pride –
We are named to march unblooded to the winning of a nation,
And to crown her with a glory that may evermore abide.

Have ye looked to great old nations, have ye wondered at their making,
Seen their fair and gracious cities, gemmed with palaces of light,
Felt the pulse of mighty engines beating ever, never slaking,
Like the sandalled feet of Progress moving onward in the night?
Can ye stand on some high headland when the drowsy day is fading,
And in dreamlike fancy see a merchant fleet upon the seas,
See the pinioned ships majestic 'gainst the purple even sailing
And the busy steamers racing down to half a thousand quays?

Have ye dreamed of this or seen of this, and feel ye no elation
O'er the most heroic duty that a free-born people knows?
To the chain of kindred nations ours to link another nation,
Ours to stay and build and bless her for a future great as those!
Cold and sordid hearts may linger still to bargain over trifles,
But the big-souled men have only hate for huckstering and sloth;

These would batter down division, tear away the bonds that stifle,
And would free our dear Australia for the larger, nobler growth.

Bushmen, roaming on the ridges, tracking – colours – to their sources,
Swinging axes by the rivers where the millsaws rend and shriek
Smoking thoughtful pipes, or dreaming on your slow, untroubled horses,
While the lazy cattle feed along the track or ford the creek,
Ye have known our country's moods in all her wild and desert places,
Ye have felt the sweet, strange promptings that her solitudes inspire;
To have breathed the spirit of her is to love her – turn your faces,
Ride like lovers when the day dawns, ride to serve her, son and sire!

Miners in the dripping workings, farmers, pioneers who settle
On the bush lands, city workers of the benches and the marts,
Swart mechanics at the forges, beating out the glowing metal,
Thinkers, planners, if ye feel the love of country stir your hearts,
Help to write the bravest chapter of a fair young nation's story
Great she'll be as Europe's greatest, more magnificent in truth!
That our children's children standing in the rose light of her glory
May all honour us who loved her, and who crowned her in her youth!

---

*slake* = usually means 'to quench a thirst',
but poetically means 'to moderate'
*swart* = swarthy

# THE WOMEN OF THE WEST

### George Essex Evans

They left the vine-wreathed cottage and the mansion on the hill,
The houses in the busy streets where life is never still,
The pleasures of the city, and the friends they cherished best:
For love they faced the wilderness – the Women of the West.

The roar, and rush, and fever of the city died away,
And the old-time joys and faces – they were gone for many a day;
In their place the lurching coach-wheel, or the creaking bullock chains,
O'er the everlasting sameness of the never-ending plains.

In the slab-built, zinc-roofed homestead of some lately taken run,
In the tent beside the bankment of a railway just begun,
In the huts on new selections, in the camps of man's unrest,
On the frontiers of the Nation, live the Women of the West.

The red sun robs their beauty, and, in weariness and pain,
The slow years steal the nameless grace that never comes again;
And there are hours men cannot soothe, and words men cannot say –
The nearest woman's face may be a hundred miles away.

The wide bush holds the secrets of their longing and desires,
When the white stars in reverence light their holy altar fires,
And silence, like the touch of God, sinks deep into the breast –
Perchance He hears and understands the Women of the West.

For them no trumpet sounds the call, no poet plies his arts –
They only hear the beating of their gallant, loving hearts.
But they have sung with silent lives the song all songs above –
The holiness of sacrifice, the dignity of love.

Well have we held our father's creed. No call has passed us by.
We faced and fought the wilderness, we sent our sons to die.
And we have hearts to do and dare, and yet, o'er all the rest,
The hearts that made the Nation were the Women of the West.

George Essex Evans (1863–1909) emigrated from
his native Wales to Queensland when he was
seventeen and ultimately settled in Toowomba.

# TURN-OF-THE-CENTURY BLUES

While many rejoiced at the creation of a new nation, others viewed these events in a more jaundiced way. Henry Lawson lamented that the celebrations were being led by English aristocrats. Many other *Bulletin* Bards were contrarian, as can be seen from the considerable difference in tone between Edward Dyson's vision of the 'Women of the West' and Victor Daley's 'The Woman at the Washtub'.

A mood of disillusionment engulfed the poets, now in their middle age, and feeling it. But no one could match the disillusionment of Breaker Morant facing his firing squad. The Boer War – or the Second Boer War, as it is more properly called – had broken out in 1899. As befitted the jingoism of those times, Australia rushed to lend a hand in support of the British Empire. This conflict cast a pall over the turn of the century and did not conclude until 1902, by which time the poet Breaker Morant had become one of its more notable casualties.

# THE MEN WHO MADE AUSTRALIA
## (WRITTEN ON THE OCCASION OF THE ROYAL VISIT TO AUSTRALIA, 1901)

### *Henry Lawson*


There'll be royal times in Sydney for the Cuff and Collar Push,
  There'll be lots of dreary drivel and clap-trap
From the men who own Australia, but who never knew the Bush,
  And who could not point their runs out on the map.
O the daily Press will grovel as it never did before,
  There'll be many flags of welcome in the air,
And the Civil Service poet, he shall write odes by the score –
  But the men who made the land will not be there.

You shall meet the awful Lady of the latest Birthday Knight –
  (She is trying to be English, don't-cher-know?)
You shall hear the empty mouthing of the champion blatherskite,
  You shall hear the boss of local drapers blow.
There'll be 'majahs' from the counter, tailors' dummies from the fleet,
  And to represent Australia here to-day
There's the toady with his card-case and his cab in Downing-street;
  But the men who made Australia – where are they?

Call across the blazing sand wastes of the Never-Never Land!
  There are some who will not answer yet awhile;

Some whose bones rot in the mulga or lie bleaching on the sand,
    Died of thirst to win the land another mile.
Thrown from horses, ripped by cattle, lost on deserts; and the weak,
    Mad through loneliness or drink (no matter which),
Drowned in floods or dead of fever by the sluggish slimy creek –
    These are men who died to make the Wool-Kings rich.

Call across the scrubby ridges where they clear the barren soil,
    And the gaunt Bushwomen share the work of men –
Toil and loneliness for ever – hardship, loneliness and toil –
    Where the brave drought-ruined farmer starts again!
Call across the boundless sheep-runs of a country cursed for sheep –
    Call across the awful scrublands west of Bourke!
But they have no time to listen – they have scarcely time to sleep –
    For the men who conquer deserts have to work.

Dragged behind the crawling sheep-flock on the hot and dusty plain,
    They must make a cheque to feed the wife and kids –
Riding night-watch round the cattle in the pelting, freezing rain,
    While world-weariness is pressing down the lids.
And away on far out-stations, seldom touched by Heaven's breath,
    In a loneliness that smothers love and hate –
Where they never take white women – there they live the living death
    With a half-caste or a black-gin for a mate.

They must toil to save the gaunt stock in the blazing months of drought,
    When the stinging, blinding blight is in men's eyes –
On the wretched, burnt selections, on the big runs further out
    Where the sand-storm rises lurid to the skies.

Not to profit when the grass is waving waist-high after rain,
    And the mighty clip of wool comes rolling in –
For the Wool-King goes to Paris with his family again
    And the gold that souls are sacrificed to win.

There are carriages in waiting for the swells from over-sea,
    There are banquets in the latest London style,
While the men who made Australia live on damper, junk and tea –
    But the quiet voices whisper, 'Wait a while!'
For the sons of all Australia, they were born to conquer fate –
    And, where charity and friendship are sincere,
Where a sinner is a brother and a stranger is a mate,
    There the future of a nation's written clear.

Aye, the cities claim the triumphs of a land they do not know,
    But all empty is the day they celebrate!
For the men who made Australia federated long ago,
    And the men to rule Australia – they can wait.
Though the bed may be the rough bunk or the gum leaves or the sand,
    And the roof for half the year may be the sky –
There are men amongst the Bushmen who were born to save the land!
    And they'll take their places sternly by-and-by.

There's a whisper on the desert though the sunset breeze hath died
    In the scrubs, though not a breath to stir a bough,
There's a murmur, not of waters, down the Lachlan River side,
    'Tis the spirit of Australia waking now!
There's the weird hymn of the drought-night on the western water-shed,
    Where the beds of unlocked rivers crack and parch;

'Tis the dead that we have buried, and our great unburied dead,
   Who are calling now on living men to march!

Round the camp fire of the fencers by the furthest panel west,
   In the men's hut by the muddy billabong,
On the Great North-Western Stock-routes where the drovers never rest,
   They are sorting out the right things from the wrong.
In the shearers' hut the slush lamp shows a haggard, stern-faced man
   Preaching war against the Wool-King to his mates;
And wherever go the billy, water-bag and frying-pan,
   They are drafting future histories of states!

# THE WOMAN AT THE WASHTUB

*Victor Daley*

The Woman at the Washtub,
  She works till fall of night;
With soap and suds and soda
  Her hands are wrinkled white.
Her diamonds are the sparkles
  The copper-fire supplies;
Her opals are the bubbles
  That from the suds arise.

The Woman at the Washtub
  Has lost the charm of youth;
Her hair is rough and homely,
  Her figure is uncouth;
Her temper is like thunder,
  With no one she agrees –
The children of the alley
  They cling around her knees.

The Woman at the Washtub,
  She too had her romance;
There was a time when lightly
  Her feet flew in the dance.
Her feet were silver swallows,
  Her lips were flowers of fire;

Then she was Bright and Early,
   The Blossom of Desire.

O Woman at the Washtub,
   And do you ever dream
Of all your days gone by in
   Your aureole of steam?
From birth till we are dying
   You wash our sordid duds,
O Woman of the Washtub!
   O Sister of the Suds!

Victor Daley (1858–1905) was born in Ireland and is
notable as the first Australian author to try to earn a
living from his writing. Much of his poetry is nostalgic for
the Celtic Twilight; little of it resonates today. These are
the first four verses of a six-verse evocation of a woman
who would have been very familiar to his readers.

# STATION LIFE

**W.T. Goodge**

Oh, a station life is the life for me,
  And the cold baked mutton in the morning!
Oh, the glorious ride o'er the plains so free,
  And the cold baked mutton in the morning!
And the rising moon on the mountain's brow!
And the ringtailed 'possum on the gum tree bough!
And the leathery damper and the salted cow,
  And the cold baked mutton in the morning!

# DAMN

*Anonymous*

Damn Coolgardie, damn the track,
Damn it there and damn it back;
Damn the country, damn the weather –
Damn the goldfields altogether!

---

This small but passionate outburst of disillusionment
at Coolgardie apparently dates back to the
1880s. It was collected by Warren Fahey.

# BOURKE

### *Henry Lawson*

I've followed all my tracks and ways, from old bark school to Leicester Square,
I've been right back to boyhood's days, and found no light or pleasure there.
But every dream and every track – and there were many that I knew –
They all lead on, or they lead back, to Bourke in Ninety-one, and two.

No sign that green grass ever grew in scrubs that blazed beneath the sun;
The plains were dust in Ninety-two, that baked to bricks in Ninety-one.
On glaring iron-roofs of Bourke, the scorching, blinding sandstorms blew,
And there was nothing beautiful in Ninety-one and Ninety-two.

Save grit and generosity of hearts that broke and healed again –
The hottest drought that ever blazed could never parch the hearts of men;
And they were men in spite of all, and they were straight, and they were true,
The hat went round at trouble's call, in Ninety-one and Ninety-two.

They drank, when all is said and done, they gambled, and their speech was rough –
You'd only need to say of one – 'He was my mate!' that was enough.
To hint a bushman was not white, nor to his Union straight and true,
Would mean a long and bloody fight in Ninety-one and Ninety-two.

The yard behind the Shearers' Arms was reckoned best of battle grounds,
And there in peace and quietness they fought their ten or fifteen rounds;
And then they washed the blood away, and then shook hands, as strong men do –
And washed away the bitterness – in Ninety-one and Ninety-two.

The Army on the grand old creek was mighty in those days gone by,
For they had sisters who could shriek, and brothers who could testify;
And by the muddy waterholes, they tackled sin till all was blue –
They took our bobs and damned our souls in Ninety-one and Ninety-two.

By shanty bars and shearing sheds, they took their toll and did their work –
But now and then they lost their heads, and raved of hotter hells than Bourke:
The only message from the dead that ever came distinctly through –
Was – 'Send my overcoat to hell' – it came to Bourke in Ninety-two.

These are the first seven verses from Lawson's
much longer poem of disillusionment.

# WHEN BILLY SINGS "THE WILD COLONIAL BOY"

## Alfred Chandler

When the pipes are all a-glowing
And the sheep are in the break,
If the day has not been over hard and long;
Then the yarns are set a-going,
And the birds are kept awake
By a burst of sound the drovers call a song,
It is not exactly restful,
Yet it's strenuous and zestful,
Though the eighteenth verse is somewhat apt to cloy;
But I don't resent it greatly,
I can sit there quite sedately
Until Billy sings "The Wild Colonial Boy."

There are songs of British valour
(Twenty verses – all alike),
And a battle where the British win the day;
There's a maid whose waxen pallor
(This is one you're bound to strike),
Touched a villain who was leading her astray,
They are marvellous and strong,
And sometimes they're rather long,
Though they mostly lack the power to annoy;

But my heart is filled with sadness,
Or with wrath akin to madness,
When Billy sings "The Wild Colonial Boy."

It is dangerous to grumble,
So I rise and sadly stumble
To my swag – spread out to leeward of the dray;
And the singer's days I number
As I seek the land of slumber
Till the sweet voice of the singer fades away;
But that ballad – unforgiven –
Haunts my dreams; while, discord-riven,
My heart throbs with a wild, unholy joy –
Round his throat my fingers tangle,
And – in dreams – I slowly strangle
The man who sings "The Wild Colonial Boy."

---

Alfred Chandler was born in Geelong in 1852. While in
Adelaide he co-founded the satirical weekly, *Quiz*, in 1892.
He went to the Coolgardie goldrush and edited a number of
Western Australian newspapers. He died in Perth in 1941,
having been a prominent member of the secession movement
there. This, his best-known poem, was published in *The Bulletin*
on 28 January 1904 under his usual pseudonym, 'Spinifex'.

# ME AND MY DOG

*Anonymous*

Me and my dog
have tramped together
in cold weather
and hot.

Me and my dog
don't care whether
we get any work
or not.

# AUSTRALIA
## (IN CONTEMPORARY LITERATURE)

### *R.H. Croll*

Whalers, damper, swag and nosebag, Johnny-cakes and billy-tea
Murrumburrah, Meremendicoowoke, Yoularbudgeree,
Cattle-duffers, bold bushrangers, diggers, drovers, bush race-courses,
And on all the other pages horses, horses, horses, horses.

In 1899, A.G. Stephens persuaded *The Bulletin's* management
to launch a literary journal, *The Bookfellow,* and in its May issue
of that year he invited his readers to contribute 'a quatrain
describing and embodying Australia'. This was how the poet and
critic Bob Croll (1869–1947) irreverently summarised the subject
matter of Australian poetry at the close of the nineteenth century.

# BUTCHERED TO MAKE A DUTCHMAN'S HOLIDAY

### *Breaker Morant*

In prison cell I sadly sit,
A d——d crest-fallen chappie!
And own to you I feel a bit –
  A little bit – unhappy!

It really ain't the place nor time
To reel off rhyming diction –
  But yet we'll write a final rhyme
While waiting cru-ci-fixion!

No matter what "end" they decide –
  Quick-lime or "b'iling ile", sir ?
We'll do our best when crucified
To finish off in style, sir!

But we bequeath a parting tip
For sound advice of such men
  Who come across in transport ship
To polish off the Dutchmen!

If you encounter any Boers
  You really must not loot 'em!

And, if you wish to leave these shores,
For pity's sake, DON'T SHOOT 'EM!

And if you'd earn a D.S.O.,
Why every British sinner
Should know the proper way to go
Is: "ASK THE BOER TO DINNER!"

Let's toss a bumper down our throat,
Before we pass to Heaven,
And toast: "The trim-set petticoat
We leave behind in Devon."

---

Harry Harbord Morant (9 December 1864–27 February 1902)
was an Anglo-Australian drover and soldier, whose skill
with horses earned him the nickname 'The Breaker'. As a
renowned poet, the bulk of his work appeared in *The Bulletin*.

His last months are immortalised in Bruce Beresford's popular
film, *Breaker Morant* (1980). He was controversially court-
martialled for murdering Boer prisoners of war, together with
a German missionary who had witnessed that atrocity.

This poem appeared in *The Bulletin* of 19 April 1902, almost two
months after Morant's execution, exactly as reproduced here.
In its manuscript version it is described as 'The Last Rhyme and
Testament of Tony Lumpkin' and it was subsequently republished
under the alternative title, 'In a Prison Cell I Sadly Sit'.

# THE PIOUS CERTAINTIES
# OF JOHN O'BRIEN

Father Patrick Joseph Hartigan (1878–1952), during the most significant part of his life, was the much-loved parish priest at Narrandera in southern New South Wales, beginning in 1916. He had been born in Yass; his first posting was seven years at Albury, where he was one of the first curates to drive a motor car. In 1911 he took the last sacraments to Jack Riley of Bringenbrong, said to have been the original Man from Snowy River.

In 1906 Hartigan began publishing verse, including in *The Bulletin*. Encouraged by George Robertson, C.J. Dennis and others, he published *Around the Boree Log and Other Verses*, under the pseudonym 'John O'Brien', in November 1921. As the *Australian Dictionary of Biography* states: 'Recording with humour and pathos the lively faith, solid piety and everyday lives of the people around him, Hartigan successfully combined the old faith of Ireland with the mateship and ethos of the bush, towards the end of an age when the small selectors and squatters went by sulky or shandrydan to The Church Upon the Hill.'

Although the bulk of Father Hartigan's poetry was composed and published after the Great War, it is included here because to some extent it is the last great expression of the old bush tradition and, at its best, is an inspired evocation of the lives and values he and his fellow poets cherished before the modern world made them seem old-fashioned.

# AROUND THE BOREE LOG

### *John O'Brien*

Oh, stick me in the old caboose this night of wind and rain,
And let the doves of fancy loose to bill and coo again.
I want to feel the pulse of love that warmed the blood like wine;
I want to see the smile above this kind old land of mine.

So come you by your parted ways that wind the wide world through,
And make a ring around the blaze the way we used to do;
The "fountain" on the sooted crane will sing the old, old song
Of common joys in homely vein forgotten, ah, too long.

*The years have turned the rusted key, and time is on the jog,*
*Yet spend another night with me around the boree log.*

Now someone driving through the rain will happen in, I bet;
So fill the fountain up again, and leave the table set.
For this was ours with pride to say – and all the world defy –
No stranger ever turned away, no neighbour passed us by.

Bedad, he'll have to stay the night; the rain is going to pour –
So make the rattling windows tight, and close the kitchen door,
And bring the old lopsided chair, the tattered cushion, too –
We'll make the stranger happy there, the way we used to do.

*The years have turned the rusted key, and time is on the jog,*
*Yet spend another night with me around the boree log.*

He'll fill his pipe, and good and well, and all aglow within
We'll hear the news he has to tell, the yarns he has to spin;
Yarns-yes, and super-yarns, forsooth, to set the eyes agog,
And freeze the blood of trusting youth around the boree log.

Then stir it up and make it burn; the poker's next to you;
Come, let us poke it all in turn, the way we used to do.
There's many a memory bright and fair will tingle at a name –
But leave unstirred the embers there we cannot fan to flame.

*For years have turned the rusted key, and time is on the jog;*
*Still, spend this fleeting night with me around the boree log.*

---

*caboose* = most commonly the guard's van on the back of a goods
train, in the country this can also be a modest hut
*Boree Log* = the Aboriginal name for the wood of the Weeping
Myall. In Father Hartigan's estimation, it was 'the best firewood
in Australia except Gidgee'.
*the fountain* = a large iron vessel of boiling water, hanging off a
crane-like projection above the fire with its lid tunefully rattling

# AT CASEY'S AFTER MASS

### John O'Brien

There's a weather-beaten sign-post where the track turns towards the west,
Through the tall, white, slender timber, in the land I love the best.
Short its message is – "To Casey's" – for it points the road to Casey's;
And my homing heart goes bushwards on an idle roving quest,
Down the old, old road contented, o'er the gum-leaves crisp and scented,
Where a deft hand splashed the purple on the big hill's sombre crest.
Ah, it's long, long years and dreary, many, many steps and weary,
Back to where the lingering dew of morn bedecked the barley-grass,
When I watched the wild careering of the neighbours through the clearing
Down that sweet bush track to Casey's, o'er the paddock down to Casey's;
Spending Sunday down at Casey's after Mass.

For, as soon as Mass was over, round the church they swarmed like bees,
Filled their pipes and duly lit them, brushed the dust from off their knees;
Then they'd "ready-up" for Casey's – self-invited down to Casey's –
Harness horses for the women with a bushman's careless ease.
With a neat spring to the saddle, soon would start the wild skedaddle.
Passing gigs and traps and buggies packed as tight as they could squeeze;
Hearts as buoyant as a feather in the mellow autumn weather,
While the noisy minahs cheered to see the glad procession pass –
All the Regans and the Ryans, and the whole mob of O'Briens
Bringing up the rear to Casey's – in the Shandrydan to Casey's –
Spending Sunday down at Casey's after Mass.

Past the kitchen door they rattled and they took the horses out;
While the women went inside at once, the menfolk hung about
Round the stable down at Casey's, waiting dinner down at Casey's;
And they talked about the Government, and blamed it for the drought,
Sitting where the sunlight lingers, picking splinters from their fingers,
Settling all the problems of the world beyond a chance of doubt.
From inside there came the bustle of the cheerful wholesome hustle,
As dear old Mrs. Casey tried all records to surpass;
Oh, there's many a memory blesses her sweet silver-braided tresses;
They were "lovely" down at Casey's – always joking down at Casey's –
Spending Sunday down at Casey's after Mass.

So they called us in to dinner, five-and-twenty guests – and more –
At the longest kitchen-table ever stood upon a floor.
There was plenty down at Casey's – ay, an open house was Casey's,
Where the neighbour and his missus never, never passed the door;
Where they counted kindly giving half the joy and pride of living
And the seasons came full-handed, and the angels blessed the store;
While the happy Laughing Mary flitted round us like a fairy.
And the big, shy boys stopped business, and looked up to watch her pass –
Ah, but when she caught them staring at the ribbons she was wearing!
Well, they spilled their tea at Casey's – on the good clean cloth at Casey's –
Spending Sunday down at Casey's after Mass.

Then the reckless feats of daring, and the bushman's fierce delight
When the brumby squealed and rooted, and the saddle-girths were tight!
They could ride 'em down at Casey's – stick like plasters down at Casey's –
When they noticed Mary looking, they would go with all their might;
Ho! they belted, and they clouted, and they yelled, and whooped, and shouted,

"Riding flash" to "ketch" the ladies, spurring, flogging, left and right!
And the lad with manners airy risked his neck for Laughing Mary
When he summoned all his courage up a rival to surpass;
Oh, the fun went fast and faster, as he landed in disaster
In the puddle-hole at Casey's – with his brand new suit at Casey's –
Spending Sunday down at Casey's after Mass.

Hoary, hale, bewhiskered veterans, perched like mopokes in a row,
 Out of danger on the top-rail, gave advice to those below;
They were wonders down at Casey's, were the old men at the Caseys' –
They're the boys could ride the "bad 'uns" in the days of long ago!
Faith, and old man Casey told 'em of a way he had to hold 'em.
Man, "the deuce an outlaw thrun him", when he "got a proper show";
Ay, and each man "upped and showed 'em" how he "handled 'em, an' rode 'em" –
Pshaw! there never was a native these old riders could outclass.
Once again they were "among 'em", and they "roped 'em" and they "slung 'em"
On the stockyard fence at Casey's – smoking, pitchin', down at Casey's –
Spending Sunday down at Casey's after Mass.

Hard and cold is youth to fancies which around the old men cling;
So they left them perched upon the rail to swap their vapouring,
Took a seat inside at Casey's, on the good chairs at the Casey's;
While the Casey's new piano made the old house rock and ring.
There their mild eyes stared and glistened, as they sat around and listened
To the tuneful little ditties Laughing Mary used to sing;
There they rubbed their chins and reckoned that to no one was she second –
"Cripes, she'd sing the blooming head off any singer in her class!"
And the banter and the laughter when the chorus hit the rafter!
It was "great" to be at Casey's – healthy, wholesome fun at Casey's –
Spending Sunday down at Casey's after Mass.

There was something in the old life which I cannot quite forget;
There are happy golden memories that hover round me yet –
Something special down at Casey's, in that wonderland of Casey's,
Where the crowfoot and the clover spread a downy coverlet,
Where the trees seemed always greener, where the life of man was cleaner,
And the joys that grew around us shed no leaves of brown regret.
oh, the merry, merry party! oh, the simple folk and hearty,
Who can fling their cares behind them, and forget them while they pass
Simple lives and simple pleasure never stinted in the measure.
There was something down at Casey's, something clean and good at Casey's –
Spending Sunday down at Casey's after Mass.

Passed and gone that old bush homestead where the hours too swiftly flew;
Silent now the merry voices of the happy friends I knew;
We have drifted far from Casey's. All deserted now is Casey's –
Just a lone brick chimney standing, and a garden-tree or two.
Still the minahs love to linger where the sign-post points the finger
Down the bush track winding westward where the tall white timber grew.
But the big hill seems to wonder why the ties are snapped asunder,
Why the neighbours never gather, never loiter as they pass;
Yet a tear-stained thought beseeming comes along and sets me dreaming
That I'm back again at Casey's, with the old, old friends at Casey's;
Spending Sunday down at Casey's after Mass.

# SAID HANRAHAN

### John O'Brien

"We'll all be rooned," said Hanrahan,
  In accents most forlorn,
Outside the church, ere Mass began,
  One frosty Sunday morn.

The congregation stood about,
  Coat-collars to the ears,
And talked of stock, and crops, and drought,
  As it had done for years.

"It's looking crook," said Daniel Croke;
  "Bedad, it's cruke, me lad,
For never since the banks went broke
  Has seasons been so bad."

"It's dry, all right," said young O'Neil,
  With which astute remark
He squatted down upon his heel
  And chewed a piece of bark.

And so around the chorus ran
  "It's keepin' dry, no doubt."
"We'll all be rooned," said Hanrahan,
  "Before the year is out."

"The crops are done; ye'll have your work
   To save one bag of grain;
From here way out to Back-o'-Bourke
   They're singin' out for rain.

"They're singin' out for rain," he said,
   "And all the tanks are dry."
The congregation scratched its head,
   And gazed around the sky.

"There won't be grass, in any case,
   Enough to feed an ass;
There's not a blade on Casey's place
   As I came down to Mass."

"If rain don't come this month," said Dan,
   And cleared his throat to speak –
"We'll all be rooned," said Hanrahan,
   "If rain don't come this week."

A heavy silence seemed to steal
   On all at this remark;
And each man squatted on his heel,
   And chewed a piece of bark.

"We want an inch of rain, we do,"
   O'Neil observed at last;
But Croke "maintained" we wanted two
   To put the danger past.

"If we don't get three inches, man,
  Or four to break this drought,
We'll all be rooned," said Hanrahan,
  "Before the year is out."

In God's good time down came the rain;
  And all the afternoon
On iron roof and window-pane
  It drummed a homely tune.

And through the night it pattered still,
  And lightsome, gladsome elves
On dripping spout and window-sill
  Kept talking to themselves.

It pelted, pelted all day long,
  A-singing at its work,
Till every heart took up the song
  Way out to Back-o'-Bourke.

And every creek a banker ran,
  And dams filled overtop;
"We'll all be rooned," said Hanrahan,
  "If this rain doesn't stop."

And stop it did, in God's good time;
  And spring came in to fold
A mantle o'er the hills sublime
  Of green and pink and gold.

And days went by on dancing feet,
  With harvest-hopes immense,
And laughing eyes beheld the wheat
  Nid-nodding o'er the fence.

And, oh, the smiles on every face,
  As happy lad and lass
Through grass knee-deep on Casey's place
  Went riding down to Mass.

While round the church in clothes genteel
  Discoursed the men of mark,
And each man squatted on his heel,
  And chewed his piece of bark.

"There'll be bush-fires for sure, me man,
  There will, without a doubt;
We'll all be rooned," said Hanrahan,
  "Before the year is out."

# PRESBYT'RY DOG

### John O'Brien

Now of all the old sinners in mischief immersed,
From the ages of Gog and Magog,
At the top of the list, from the last to the first,
And by every good soul in the parish accursed,
Is that scamp of a Presbyt'ry Dog.

He's a hairy old scoundrel as ugly as sin,
He's a demon that travels incog.,
With a classical name, and an ignorant grin,
And a tail, by the way, that is scraggy and thin,
And the rest of him merely a dog.

He is like a young waster of fortune possessed,
As he rambles the town at a jog;
For he treats the whole world as a sort of a jest,
While the comp'ny he keeps – well, it must be confessed
It's unfit for a Presbyt'ry Dog.

He is out on the street at the sound of a fight,
With the eyes on him standing agog,
And the scut of a tail – well, bedad, it's a fright;
Faith, you'd give him a kick that would set him alight,
But you can't with the Presbyt'ry Dog.

His rotundity now to absurdity runs,
Like a blackfellow gone to the grog;
For the knowing old shaver the presbyt'ry shuns
When its time for a meal, and goes off to the nuns,
Who're deceived in the Presbyt'ry Dog.

When he follows the priest to the bush, there is war.
He inspects the whole place at a jog,
And he puts on great airs and fine antics galore,
While he chases the sheep till we're after his gore,
Though he may be the Presbyt'ry Dog.

'Twas last Sunday a dog in the church went ahead
With an ill-bred and loud monologue,
And the priest said some things that would shiver the dead,
And I'm with him in every last word that he said –
Ah, but wait – 'twas the Presbyt'ry Dog.

---

*scut* = a short, erect tail

# TANGMALANGALOO

## *John O'Brien*

The bishop sat in lordly state and purple cap sublime,
And galvanized the old bush church at Confirmation time;
And all the kids were mustered up from fifty miles around,
With Sunday clothes, and staring eyes, and ignorance profound.
Now was it fate, or was it grace, whereby they yarded too
An overgrown two-storey lad from Tangmalangaloo?

A hefty son of virgin soil, where nature has had her fling,
And grows the trefoil three feet high and mats it in the spring;
Where mighty hills uplift their heads to pierce the welkin's rim,
And trees sprout up a hundred feet before they shoot a limb;
There everything is big and grand, and men are giants too –
But Christian Knowledge wilts, alas, at Tangmalangaloo.

The bishop summed the youngsters up, as bishops only can;
He cast a searching glance around, then fixed upon his man.
But glum and dumb and undismayed through every bout he sat;
He seemed to think that he was there, but wasn't sure of that.
The bishop gave a scornful look, as bishops sometimes do,
And glared right through the pagan in from Tangmalangaloo.

'Come, tell me, boy,' his lordship said, in crushing tones severe,
'Come, tell me why is Christmas Day the greatest of the year?
'How is it that around the world we celebrate that day

'And send a name upon a card to those who're far away?
'Why is it wandering ones return with smiles and greetings, too?'
A squall of knowledge hit the lad from Tangmalangaloo.

He gave a lurch which set a-shake the vases on the shelf,
He knocked the benches all askew, up-ending of himself.
And so, how pleased his lordship was, and how he smiled to say,
'That's good, my boy. Come, tell me now; and what is Christmas Day?'
The ready answer bared a fact no bishop ever knew –
'It's the day before the races out at Tangmalangaloo.'

---

*welkin* = a literary word for the sky

# THE OLD BUSH SCHOOL

### John O'Brien

'Tis a queer, old battered landmark that belongs to other years;
With the dog-leg fence around it, and its hat about its ears,
And the cow-bell in the gum-tree, and the bucket on the stool,
There's a motley host of memories round that old bush school –

With its seedy desks and benches, where at least I left a name
Carved in agricultural letters – 'twas my only bid for fame;
And the spider-haunted ceilings, and the rafters, firmly set,
Lined with darts of nibs and paper (doubtless sticking in them yet),
And the greasy slates and blackboards, where I oft was proved a fool
And a blur upon the scutcheon of the old bush school.

There I see the boots in order – "'lastic-sides" we used to wear –
With a pair of "everlastin's" cracked and dusty here and there;
And we marched with great "high action" – hands behind and eyes before –
While we murdered *Swanee River* as we tramped around the floor.

Still the scholars pass before me with their freckled features grave,
And a nickname fitting better than the name their mothers gave;
Tousled hair and vacant faces, and their garments every one
Shabby heirlooms in the family, handed down from sire to son.
Ay, and mine were patched in places, and half-masted, as a rule –
They were fashionable trousers at the old bush school.

There I trudged it from the Three-mile, like a patient, toiling brute,
With a stocking round my ankle, and my heart within my boot,
Morgan, Nell and Michael Joseph, Jim and Mary, Kate and Mart
Tramping down the sheep-track with me, little rebels at the heart;
Shivery grasses round about us nodding bonnets in the breeze,
Happy Jacks and Twelve Apostles hurdle-racing up the trees,
Peewees calling from the gullies, living wonders in the pool –
Hard bare seats and drab gray humdrum at the old bush school.

Early rising in the half-light, when the morn came, bleak and chill;
For the little mother roused us ere the sun had topped the hill,
"Up, you children, late 'tis gettin'." Shook the house beneath her knock,
And she wasn't always truthful, and she tampered with the clock.

Keen she was about "the learnin'", and she told us o'er and o'er
Of our luck to have "the schoolin'" right against our very door.
And the lectures – Oh, those lectures to our stony hearts addressed!
"Don't be mixin' with the Regans and the Ryans and the rest" –
"Don't be pickin' up with Carey's little talkative kanats" –
Well, she had us almost thinking we were born aristocrats.
But we found our level early – in disaster, as a rule –
For they knocked "the notions" sideways at the old bush school.

Down the road came Laughing Mary, and the beast that she bestrode
Was Maloney's sorry piebald she had found beside the road;
Straight we scrambled up behind her, and as many as could fit
Clung like circus riders bare-back without bridle-rein or bit,
On that corrugated backbone in a merry row we sat –
We propelled him with our school-bags; Mary steered him with her hat –

And we rolled the road behind us like a ribbon from the spool,
"Making butter", so we called it, to the old bush school.

What a girl was Mary Casey in the days of long ago!
She was queen among the scholars, or at least we thought her so;
She was first in every mischief and, when overwhelmed by fate,
She could make delightful drawings of the teacher on her slate.
There was rhythm in every movement, as she gaily passed along
With a rippling laugh that lilted like the music of a song;
So we called her "Laughing Mary", and a fitful fancy blessed
E'en the bashful little daisies that her dainty feet caressed.

She had cheeks like native roses in the fullness of their bloom,
And she used to sing the sweetest as we marched around the room;
In her eyes there lurked the magic, maiden freshness of the morn,
In her hair the haunting colour I had seen upon the corn;
Round her danced the happy sunshine when she smiled upon the stool –
And I used to swap her dinners at the old bush school.

Hard the cobbled road of knowledge to the feet of him who plods
After fragile fragments fallen from the workshop of the gods;
Long the quest, and ever thieving pass the pedlars o'er the hill
With the treasures in their bundles, but to leave us questing still.
Mystic fires horizons redden, but each crimson flash in turn
Only lights the empty places in the bracken and the fern;
So in after years I've proved it, spite of pedant, crank, and fool,
Very much the way I found it at the old bush school.

. . . over

*scutcheon* = variant of 'escutcheon', a posh word for one's good name (as in 'a blot on your escutcheon')

*Swanee River* = the alternative name for Stephen Foster's evergreen song, 'Old Folks At Home'

*stocking* = sock

*Happy Jacks* = Grey-crowned Babblers, which are brown with white markings

*Twelve Apostles* = Apostle Birds, grey with brown wings

*kanat* = apparently a corruption of the word 'gnat', meaning here undersized, mischievous, useless and perky

# TEN LITTLE STEPS AND STAIRS

### John O'Brien

There were ten little Steps and Stairs
  Round through the old bush home all day
  Romping about in the old bush way.
They were ten little wild March hares,
  Storming the kitchen in hungry lines,
  With their naked feet, doing mud designs,
  "All over the place like punkin vines".
There were ten little Steps and Stairs.

There were ten little Steps and Stairs.
  In their home-made frocks and their Sunday suits,
  Up through the church with their squeaky boots,
While the folk went astray in their prayers,
  They hustled along, all dressed and neat –
  Oh, they bustled a bit as they filled the seat;
  From the first to the last, the lot complete,
There were ten little Steps and Stairs.

There were ten little Steps and Stairs.
  But the years have shuffled them all about,
  Have worn them thin, and straightened them out
With the tramp of a hundred cares;
  Ay, and each grim scar has a tale to tell
  Of a knock and a blow, and a hand that fell,

And a break in the line, and a gap. Ah, well –
There *were* ten little Steps and Stairs.

---

The sense of this poignant little poem seems to be that, for
the dutiful Catholic parent, their children were the steps
and stairs that would take them ultimately to Heaven.

# C.J. DENNIS

## A CELEBRATION OF
## THE EMERGING MODERN CITY LIFE

Clarence (Clarrie or Den) Michael James Stanislaus Dennis was born in Auburn, South Australia, on 7 September 1876. He became the best-known voice of the raucous city life then emerging. He is by far the most prolific of the great Australian poets and arguably, at the height of his powers, was the most popular. He was styled the 'Laureate of the Larrikin'.

Den may have written as many as four thousand poems. His first book, *Backblock Ballads and Other Verses*, was published in 1913 but it was the mock-heroic *The Songs of a Sentimental Bloke*, published in November 1915, that really made his reputation, selling 51,000 copies in its first nine months. *Sentimental Bloke* was published in separate editions in Britain and the United States, where it was widely appreciated. In Dennis's own lifetime it became the subject of a popular silent film (1918), a stage play (1922) and a sound film (1932); later it provided the basis for a successful musical (1961) and for a full-length production by the Australian Ballet.

Den began his working life as a publican in Adelaide where he later co-founded the weekly newspaper, *Gadfly*.

His adult life was dogged by bouts of intemperance; but he ultimately made his home at Toolangi, forty miles east of Melbourne, from where he churned out columns and verse for the Melbourne *Herald*.

In 1916, he published *The Moods of Ginger Mick* and it sold over 42,000 copies within six months. Other volumes appeared later, starring individuals from the repertory company of characters he had created. His *Glugs of Gosh* was a more serious attempt at social satire; he also collected together his verse for children under the title, *A Book for Kids*.

C.J. Dennis died on 22 June 1938 at the age of 61. He was buried in Box Hill cemetery the next day, and the inscription on his headstone was taken from his later volume, *The Singing Garden*:

*Now is the healing, quiet hour that fills*
*This gay green world with peace and grateful rest.*

The then prime minister of Australia, Joe Lyons, declared: 'I am sure that I speak for all Australians in expressing deep regret at the death of C.J. Dennis. He was the Robert Burns of Australia. He created characters which have become immortal and he captured the true Australian spirit. Already his work is world-famous, and future generations will treasure it.'

The poetry enthusiast Perry Middlemiss, one of Den's legion of modern fans, comments: 'Since his death . . . Dennis has probably fallen to third on the "classic" Australian poetry list behind Henry Lawson and Banjo Paterson. Both of these poets have appeared on Australian currency notes. It might well be time to start a campaign to have Dennis so honoured when next the Reserve Bank decides to change the ten dollar bill.'

# THE SONGS OF A SENTIMENTAL BLOKE: THREE EXCERPTS

### C.J. Dennis

## 1.    A SPRING SONG

The world 'as got me snouted jist a treat;
  Crool Forchin's dirty left 'as smote me soul;
An' all them joys o' life I 'eld so sweet
  Is up the pole.
Fer, as the poit sez, me 'eart 'as got
  The pip wiv yearnin' fer – I dunno wot.

I'm crook; me name is Mud; I've done me dash;
  Me flamin' spirit's got the flamin' 'ump!
I'm longin' to let loose on somethin' rash . . .
  Aw, I'm a chump!
I know it; but this blimed ole Springtime craze
  Fair outs me, on these dilly, silly days.

The young green leaves is shootin' on the trees,
  The air is like a long, cool swig o' beer,
The bonzer smell o' flow'rs is on the breeze,
  An' 'ere's me, 'ere,
Jist moochin' round like some pore, barmy coot,
  Of 'ope, an' joy, an' forchin destichoot.

I've lorst me former joy in gettin' shick,
  Or 'eadin' browns; I 'aven't got the 'eart
To word a tom; an', square an' all,
  I'm sick of that cheap tart
'Oo chucks 'er carkis at a feller's 'ead
  An' mauls 'im . . . Ar! I wish't that I wus dead! . . .

Ther's little breezes stirrin' in the leaves,
  An' sparrers chirpin' 'igh the 'ole day long;
An' on the air a sad, sweet music breaves
  A bonzer song –
A mournful sorter choon thet gits a bloke
  Fair in the brisket 'ere, an' makes 'im choke . . .

What is the matter wiv me? . . . I dunno.
  I got a sorter yearnin' 'ere inside,
A dead-crook sorter thing that won't let go
  Or be denied –
A feelin' like I want to do a break,
  An' stoush creation for some woman's sake.

---

snouted = rebuffed
pip = a fit of depression
outs me = knocks me out
shick = shickered, drunk
brown = a penny; 'eadin' browns = playing two-up
tom = tom-tart, a sweetheart
tart = in Dennis's world, an abbreviation of
sweetheart (later, it came to mean a prostitute)
brisket = chest
stoush = fight

## 2. 'ER NAME'S DOREEN

'Er name's Doreen . . . Well spare me bloomin' days!
You could er knocked me down wiv 'arf a brick!
  Yes, me, that kids meself I know their ways,
  An' 'as a name for smoogin' in our click!
I just lines up an' tips the saucy wink.
But strike! The way she piled on dawg! Yer'd think
  A bloke was givin' back-chat to the Queen . . .
  'Er name's Doreen.

I seen 'er in the markit first uv all,
Inspectin' brums at Steeny Isaacs' stall.
  I backs me barrer in – the same ole way –
  An' sez, "Wot O! It's been a bonzer day.
'Ow is it fer a walk?" . . . Oh, 'oly wars!
The sorter look she gimme! Jest becors
  I tried to chat 'er, like you'd make a start
  Wiv ANY tart.

An' I kin take me oaf I wus perlite.
An' never said no word that wasn't right,
  An' never tried to maul 'er, or to do
  A thing yeh might call crook. Ter tell yeh true,
I didn't seem to 'ave the nerve – wiv 'er.
I felt as if I couldn't go that fur,
  An' start to sling off chiack like I used . . .
  Not INTRAJUICED!

Nex' time I sighted 'er in Little Bourke,
Where she was in a job. I found 'er lurk
  Wus pastin' labels in a pickle joint,
  A game that – any'ow, that ain't the point.
Once more I tried ter chat 'er in the street,
But, bli'me! Did she turn me down a treat!
  The way she tossed 'er 'ead an' swished 'er skirt!
  Oh, it wus dirt!

A squarer tom, I swear, I never seen,
In all me natchril, than this 'ere Doreen.
  It wer'n't no guyver neither; fer I knoo
  That any other bloke 'ad Buckley's 'oo
Tried fer to pick 'er up. Yes, she was square.
She jist sailed by an' lef' me standin' there
  Like any mug. Thinks I, "I'm out 'er luck,"
  An' done a duck.

Well, I dunno. It's that way wiv a bloke.
If she'd ha' breasted up ter me an' spoke,
  I'd thort 'er jist a commin bit 'er fluff,
  An' then fergot about 'er, like enough.
It's jest like this. The tarts that's 'ard ter get
Makes you all 'ot to chase 'em, an' to let
  The cove called Cupid get an 'ammer-lock;
  An' lose yer block.

---

*smoogin'* = wooing
*click* = clique, one's push

. . . over

*piled on dawg* = put on the dog, i.e. put on airs
*brums* = cheap finery (from Brummagem, a
variant pronunciation of Birmingham)
*to sling off chiack* = to offer vulgar banter
*square* = honest, straightforward
*guyver* = a sham

# 3.   THE PLAY

Wot's in a name? – she sez . . . An' then she sighs,
An' clasps 'er little 'ands, an' rolls 'er eyes.
"A rose," she sez, "be any other name
Would smell the same.
Oh, w'erefore art you Romeo, young sir?
Chuck yer ole pot, an' change yer moniker!"

Doreen an' me, we bin to see a show –
The swell two-dollar touch. Bong tong, yeh know.
A chair apiece wiv velvit on the seat;
A slap-up treat.
The drarmer's writ be Shakespeare, years ago,
About a barmy goat called Romeo.

"Lady, be yonder moon I swear!" sez 'e.
An' then 'e climbs up on the balkiney;
An' there they smooge a treat, wiv pretty words
Like two love-birds.
I nudge Doreen. She whispers, "Ain't it grand!"
'Er eyes is shining an' I squeeze 'er 'and.

"Wot's in a name?" she sez. 'Struth, I dunno.
Billo is just as good as Romeo.
She may be Juli-er or Juli-et –
'E loves 'er yet.
If she's the tart 'e wants, then she's 'is queen,
Names never count . . . But ar, I like "Doreen"!

A sweeter, dearer sound I never 'eard;
Ther's music 'angs around that little word,
Doreen! . . . But wot was this I starts to say
About the play?
I'm off me beat. But when a bloke's in love
'Is thorts turns 'er way, like a 'omin' dove.

This Romeo 'e's lurkin' wiv a crew –
A dead tough crowd o' crooks – called Montague.
'Is cliner's push – wot's nicknamed Capulet –
They 'as 'em set.
Fair narks they are, jist like them back-street clicks,
Ixcep' they fights wiv skewers 'stid o' bricks.

Wot's in a name? Wot's in a string o' words?
They scraps in ole Verona wiv the'r swords,
An' never give a bloke a stray dog's chance,
An' that's Romance.
But when they deals it out wiv bricks an' boots
In Little Lon., they're low, degraded broots.

Wot's jist plain stoush wiv us, right 'ere to-day,
Is "valler" if yer fur enough away.
Some time, some writer bloke will do the trick
Wiv Ginger Mick,
Of Spadger's Lane.
'E'll be a Romeo,
When 'e's bin dead five 'undred years or so.

Fair Juli-et, she gives 'er boy the tip.
Sez she: "Don't sling that crowd o' mine no lip;
An' if you run agin a Capulet,
Jist do a get."
'E swears 'e's done wiv lash; 'e'll chuck it clean.
(Same as I done when I first met Doreen.)

They smooge some more at that. Ar, strike me blue!
It gimme Joes to sit an' watch them two!
'E'd break away an' start to say good-bye,
 An' then she'd sigh
"Ow, Ro-me-o!" an' git a strangle-holt,
An' 'ang around 'im like she feared 'e'd bolt.

Nex' day 'e words a gorspil cove about
A secret weddin'; an' they plan it out.
'E spouts a piece about 'ow 'e's bewitched:
Then they git 'itched . . .
Now, 'ere's the place where I fair git the pip!
She's 'is for keeps, an' yet 'e lets 'er slip!

Ar! but 'e makes me sick! A fair gazob!
E's jist the glarsey on the soulful sob,
'E'll sigh and spruik, a' 'owl a love-sick vow –
(The silly cow!)
But when 'e's got 'er, spliced an' on the straight
'E crools the pitch, an' tries to kid it's Fate.

Aw! Fate me foot! Instid of slopin' soon
As 'e was wed, off on 'is 'oneymoon,

'Im an' 'is cobber, called Mick Curio,
They 'ave to go
An' mix it wiv that push o' Capulets.
They look fer trouble; an' it's wot they gets.

A tug named Tyball (cousin to the skirt)
Sprags 'em an' makes a start to sling off dirt.
Nex' minnit there's a reel ole ding-dong go –
'Arf round or so.
Mick Curio, 'e gets it in the neck,
"Ar rats!" 'e sez, an' passes in 'is check.

Quite natchril, Romeo gits wet as 'ell.
"It's me or you!" 'e 'owls, an' wiv a yell,
Plunks Tyball through the gizzard wiv 'is sword,
'Ow I ongcored!
"Put in the boot!" I sez. "Put in the boot!"
"'Ush!" sez Doreen . . . "Shame!" sez some silly coot.

Then Romeo, 'e dunno wot to do.
The cops gits busy, like they allwiz do,
An' nose around until 'e gits blue funk
An' does a bunk.
They wants 'is tart to wed some other guy.
"Ah, strike!" she sez. "I wish that I could die!"

Now, this 'ere gorspil bloke's a fair shrewd 'ead.
Sez 'e "I'll dope yeh, so they'll think yer dead."
(I tips 'e was a cunnin' sort, wot knoo
A thing or two.)

She takes 'is knock-out drops, up in 'er room:
They think she's snuffed, an' plant 'er in 'er tomb.

Then things gits mixed a treat an' starts to whirl.
'Ere's Romeo comes back an' finds 'is girl
Tucked in 'er little coffing, cold an' stiff,
An' in a jiff,
'E swallows lysol, throws a fancy fit,
'Ead over turkey, an' 'is soul 'as flit.

Then Juli-et wakes up an' sees 'im there,
Turns on the water-works an' tears 'er 'air,
"Dear love," she sez, "I cannot live alone!"
An' wiv a moan,
She grabs 'is pockit knife, an' ends 'er cares . . .
"Peanuts or lollies!" sez a boy upstairs.

---

*yer ole pot* = in rhyming slang, the old 'pot 'n' pan' is
'the old man', or father
*bong tong* = 'bon ton', i.e. posh
*cliner* = a young unmarried woman
*they 'as 'em set* = they are determined to fight them
*Little Lon.* = Little Lonsdale Street, a notorious alley
*run agin* = bump into unexpectedly
*do a git* = beat a retreat
*lash* = violence
*gazob* = fool
*the glarsey on the soulful sob* = the glassy means the best,
and here he is the master of the soulful sob
*tug* = a young rowdy

. . . over

*sprag* = to accost belligerently
*to sling off dirt* = to heckle
*passes in 'is check* = dies
*gits wet* = to get angry

# A BOOK FOR KIDS: FOUR POEMS

### C.J. Dennis

## 1. HIST!

Hist! . . . . . . Hark!
The night is very dark,
And we've to go a mile or so
Across the Possum Park.

Step . . . . . . light,
Keeping to the right;
If we delay, and lose our way,
We'll be out half the night.
The clouds are low and gloomy. Oh!
It's just begun to mist!
We haven't any overcoats
And – Hist! . . . . . . Hist!

(Mo . . . . . . poke!)
Who was that that spoke?
This is not a fitting spot
To make a silly joke.

Dear . . . . . . me!
A mopoke in a tree!
It jarred me so, I didn't know

Whatever it could be.
But come along; creep along;
Soon we shall be missed.
They'll get a scare and wonder where
We – Hush! . . . . . . Hist!

Ssh! . . . . . . Soft!
I've told you oft and oft
We should not stray so far away
Without a moon aloft.

Oo! . . . . . . Scat!
Goodness! What was that?
Upon my word, it's quite absurd,
It's only just a cat.
But come along; haste along;
Soon we'll have to rush,
Or we'll be late and find the gate
Is – Hist! . . . . . . Hush!

(Kok! . . . . . . Korrock!)
Oh! I've had a shock!
I hope and trust it's only just
A frog behind a rock.

Shoo! . . . . . . Shoo!
We've had enough of you;
Scaring folk just for a joke

Is not the thing to do.
But come along, slip along –
Isn't it a lark
Just to roam so far from home
On – Hist! . . . . . . Hark!

Look! . . . . . . See!
Shining through the tree,
The window-light is glowing bright
To welcome you and me.

Shout! . . . . . . Shout!
There's someone round about,
And through the door I see some more
And supper all laid out.
Now, run! Run! Run!
Oh, we've had such splendid fun –
Through the park in the dark,
As brave as anyone.

Laughed, we did, and chaffed, we did,
And whistled all the way,
And we're home again! Home again!
Hip . . . . . . Hooray!

# 2. THE CIRCUS

Hey, there! Hoop-la! the circus is in town!
Have you seen the elephant? Have you seen the clown?
Have you seen the dappled horse gallop round the ring?
Have you seen the acrobats on the dizzy swing?
Have you seen the tumbling men tumble up and down?
Hoop-la! Hoop-la! the circus is in town!

Hey, there! Hoop-la! Here's the circus troupe!
Here's the educated dog jumping through the hoop.
See the lady Blondin with the parasol and fan,
The lad upon the ladder and the india-rubber man.
See the joyful juggler and the boy who loops the loop.
Hey! Hey! Hey! Hey! Here's the circus troupe!

---

*Blondin* = a legendary French tightrope-walker

# 3. THE TRIANTIWONTIGONGOLOPE

There's a very funny insect that you do not often spy,
And it isn't quite a spider, and it isn't quite a fly;
It is something like a beetle, and a little like a bee,
But nothing like a woolly grub that climbs upon a tree.
Its name is quite a hard one, but you'll learn it soon, I hope.
So try:
  Tri-
     Tri-anti-wonti-
      Triantiwontigongolope.

It lives on weeds and wattle-gum, and has a funny face;
Its appetite is hearty, and its manners a disgrace.
When first you come upon it, it will give you quite a scare,
But when you look for it again, you find it isn't there.
And unless you call it softly it will stay away and mope.
So try:
  Tri-
     Tri-anti-wonti-
      Triantiwontigongolope.

It trembles if you tickle it or tread upon its toes;
It is not an early riser, but it has a snubbish nose.
If you sneer at it, or scold it, it will scuttle off in shame,
But it purrs and purrs quite proudly if you call it by its name,
And offer it some sandwiches of sealing-wax and soap.
So try:  Tri-
     Tri-anti-wonti-

Triantiwontigongolope.

But of course you haven't seen it; and I truthfully confess
That I haven't seen it either, and I don't know its address.
For there isn't such an insect, though there really might have been
If the trees and grass were purple, and the sky was bottle green.
It's just a little joke of mine, which you'll forgive, I hope.
Oh, try!
  Tri-
    Tri-anti-wonti-
      Triantiwontigongolope.

# 4. WOOLLOOMOOLOO (A RIDDLE)

Here's a ridiculous riddle for you:
  How many o's are there in Woolloomooloo?
Two for the W, two for the m,
  Four for the l's, and that's plenty for them.

C.J. Dennis was captivated by riddles and by the language he heard around him in the street. Both he and W.T. Goodge were alive to the possibilities of using the Australian language and its slang in humorous verse. The next five pieces illustrate some of the potential of this poetic seam.

# AUSTRALAISE

**C.J. Dennis**

Fellers of Australier,
Blokes an' coves an' coots,
Shift yer bloody carcases,
Move yer bloody boots.
Gird yer bloody loins up,
Get yer bloody gun,
Set the bloody enermy
An' watch the blighters run.

CHORUS:
*Get a bloody move on,*
*Have some bloody sense.*
*Learn the bloody art of*
*Self de-bloody-fence.*

Have some bloody brains be-
Neath yer bloody lids.
An' swing a bloody sabre
Fer the missus an' the kids.
Chuck supportin' bloody posts,
An' strikin' bloody lights,
Support a bloody fam'ly an'
Strike fer yer bloody rights.

CHORUS:
*Get a bloody move on, &c.*

Joy is bloody fleetin',
Life is bloody short.
Wot's the use uv wastin' it
All on bloody sport?
Hitch yer bloody tip-dray
To a bloody star.
Let yer bloody watchword be
"Australi-bloody-ar!"

CHORUS:
*Get a bloody move on, &c.*

'Ow's the bloody nation
Goin' to ixpand
'Lest us bloody blokes an' coves
Lend a bloody 'and?

'Eave yer bloody apathy
Down a bloody chasm;
'Ump yer bloody burden with
Enthusi-bloody-asm.

CHORUS:
*Get a bloody move on,* &c.

Wen the bloody trouble
Hits yer native land
Take a bloody rifle
In yer bloody 'and.
Keep yer bloody upper lip
Stiff as stiff kin be,
An' speed a bloody bullet for
Pos-bloody-terity.

CHORUS:
*Get a bloody move on,* &c.

Wen the bloody bugle
Sounds "Ad-bloody-vance"
Don't be like a flock uv sheep
In a bloody trance.
Biff the bloody foeman
Where it don't agree.
Spifler-bloody-cate him
To Eternity.

CHORUS:
*Get a bloody move on,* &c.


Fellers of Australier,
Cobbers, chaps an' mates,
Hear the bloody enermy
Kickin' at the gates!
Blow the bloody bugle,
Beat the bloody drum,
Upper-cut and out the cow
To kingdom-bloody-come!

CHORUS:
*Get a bloody move on,* &c.

---

The original version of this piece won a *Bulletin* competition in 1908, but a number of other versions were produced, including one that was widely distributed during the war. It originally appeared in print with dashes replacing the offending epithet, but the above is how it appears in Jim Haynes, *The Book of Australian Rhymed Verse*.

*tip-dray* = a simple horse-drawn cart with two wheels; its contents could be tipped out of the back by raising its shaft
*spiflicate* = to destroy utterly

# THE GREAT AUSTRALIAN ADJECTIVE

## W.T. *Goodge*

A sunburnt bloody stockman stood,
And in a dismal bloody mood,
Apostrophized his bloody cuddy:
'This bloody moke's no bloody good,
He doesn't earn his bloody food.
Bloody! Bloody! Bloody!'

He jumped across his bloody horse
And galloped off of bloody course,
The road was wet and bloody muddy.
He road up hill, down bloody dale,
The wind, it blew a bloody gale.
Bloody! Bloody! Bloody!'

He came up to a bloody creek;
The bloody horse was bloody weak;
The creek was full and bloody floody.
He said, 'This moke must sink or swim,
The same for me as bloody him:
Bloody! Bloody! Bloody!'

He plunged into the bloody creek:
The horse it gave a bloody shriek:
The stockman's face a bloody study,
Ejaculating as they sank,
Before they reached the bloody bank:
'Bloody! Bloody! Bloody!'

---

When this poem was originally published, and subsequently,
'The Great Australian Adjective' was somewhat chastely
indicated by a dash. However, the variant above is the form
adopted by the poet John Kinsella in his *Anthology of Australian
Poetry to 1920*, with the expletive ejaculated thrice as the
end of each stanza. This is less mysterious to the modern
reader, who might otherwise be tempted to insert a much
stronger word and thus misconstrue which word was known
as 'The Great Australian Adjective' in Goodge's time.

*cuddy* = a small horse

# THE AUSTRALIAN SLANGUAGE

### W.T. Goodge

'Tis the everyday Australian
  Has a language of his own,
Has a language, or a slanguage,
  Which can simply stand alone.
And a "dickon pitch to kid us"
  Is a synonym for "lie",
And to "nark it" means to stop it,
  And to "nit it" means to fly.

And a bosom friend's a "cobber",
  And a horse a "prad" or "moke",
While a casual acquaintance
  Is a "joker" or a "bloke".
And his lady-love's his "donah"
  Or his "clinah" or his "tart"
Or his "little bit o' muslin",
  As it used to be his "bart".

And his naming of the coinage
  Is a mystery to some,
With his "quid" and "half-a-caser"
  And his "deener" and his "scrum".
And a "tin-back" is a party
  Who's remarkable for luck,

And his food is called his "tucker"
　　Or his "panem" or his "chuck".

A policeman is a "johnny"
　　Or a "copman" or a "trap",
And a thing obtained on credit
　　Is invariably "strap".
A conviction's known as "trouble",
　　And a gaol is called a "jug",
And a sharper is a "spieler"
　　And a simpleton's a "tug".

If he hits a man in fighting
　　That is what he calls a "plug",
If he borrows money from you
　　He will say he "bit your lug".
And to "shake it" is to steal it,
　　And to "strike it" is to beg;
And a jest is "poking borac",
　　And a jester "pulls your leg".

Things are "cronk" when they go wrongly
　　In the language of the "push",
But when things go as he wants 'em
　　He declares it is "all cush".
When he's bright he's got a "napper",
　　And he's "ratty" when he's daft,
And when looking for employment
　　He is "out o' blooming graft".

And his clothes he calls his "clobber"
  Or his "togs", but what of that
When a "castor" or a "kady"
  Is the name he gives his hat!
And our undiluted English
  Is a fad to which we cling,
But the great Australian slanguage
  Is a truly awful thing!

# THE BASTARD FROM THE BUSH

### Anonymous

As the night was falling slowly over city, town and bush,
From a slum in Jones's Alley came the Captain of the Push,
And his whistle loud and piercing woke the echoes of the Rocks,
And a dozen ghouls came slouching round the corners of the blocks.

Then the Captain jerked a finger at a stranger on the kerb
Whom he qualified politely with an adjective and verb.
Then he made the introduction: 'Here's a covey from the bush –
Fuck me blind, he wants to join us – be a member of the Push.'

Then the stranger made this answer to the Captain of the Push,
'Why, fuck you dead, I'm Foreskin Fred, the bastard from the bush.
'I've been in every two-up school from Darwin to the 'Loo,
'I've ridden colts and black gins – what more can a bastard do.'

'Are you game to smash a window?' asked the Captain of the Push.
'I'd knock a fucking house down,' said the bastard from the bush.
'Would you take a maiden's baby?' said the Captain of the Push.
'I'd take a baby's maiden,' said the bastard from the bush.

'Would you dong a bloody copper if you caught the cunt alone,
'Would you stoush a swell or Chinkee? Split his garret with a stone?
'Would you have a moll to keep you, would you swear off work for good?'
'What? Live on prostitution? My colonial oath I would!'

'Would you care to have a gasper?' said the Captain of the Push.
'I'll take the bloody packet,' said the bastard from the bush.
Then the Push-ites all took counsel, saying, 'Fuck me, but he's game.
'Let's make him our star basher, he'll live up to his name.'

So they took him to their hideout, that bastard from the bush,
And they granted him all privileges appertaining to the Push.
But soon they found his little ways were more than they could stand,
And finally the Captain thus addressed his little band.

'Now listen here, you buggers, we've caught a fucking tartar,
'At every kind of bludging, that bastard is a starter,
'At poker and at two-up, he's shook our fucking rolls,
'He swipes our fucking liquor, and he robs our fucking molls.'

So down in Jones's Alley all the members of the Push
Laid a dark and dirty ambush for the bastard from the bush.
But against the wall of Riley's pub, the bastard made a stand,
A nasty grin upon his dial, a bike-chain in each hand.

They sprang upon him in a bunch, but one by one they fell,
With crack of bone, unearthly groan, and agonising yell,
Till the sorely-battered Captain, spitting teeth and gouts of blood,
Held an ear all torn and bleeding in a hand bedaubed with mud.

'You low polluted bastard,' snarled the Captain of the Push,
'Get back to where your sort belong, that's somewhere in the bush:
'And I hope heaps of misfortune may soon tumble down on you,
'May some lousy harlot dose you till your ballocks turn sky-blue.

'May the pangs of windy spasms through your bowels dart,
'May you shit your bloody trousers every time you try to fart,
'May you take a swig of gin's piss, mistaking it for beer,
'May the next push you impose on toss you out upon your ear.

'May the itching piles torment you, may corns grow on your feet,
'May crabs as big as spiders attack your balls a treat,
'Then when you're down and outed, to a hopeless bloody wreck,
'May you slip back through your arsehole, and break your fucking neck.'

---

The 'push' was a mainly a Sydney term, meaning a company of unruly blokes gathered together for nefarious purposes. In the late-nineteenth and early-twentieth centuries, larrikins assembled in pushes, such as the Bantry Bay Devils, the Stars, the Golden Dragons, the Livers, the Forty Thieves and, perhaps the best-known of all, the Rocks Push. The term was then later reclaimed by Sydney's Andersonians in the 1950s.

This poem is sometimes attributed to Henry Lawson and there is a long-standing controversy over its authorship. Either Lawson wrote it and then cleaned it up (publishing it as 'The Captain of the Push' in *The Bulletin* of 26 March 1892), or else this is a parody of Lawson's published poem.

The best evidence against the vulgar version being Lawson's is that 'The Shearer's Dream' is as close as we know he came to composing a rude poem and it is hardly offensive. He seems to have been somewhat puritanical; for example, he never swore unless extremely drunk and agitated. However, H.A. Lindsay asserts that Lawson 'wrote the obscene version himself and circulated copies among his friends'. Later, wanting some money in a hurry, he toned it down considerably and it was published under the title of 'The Captain of the Push'. One way or another, the version above is a very well-known poem.

# "OUGH!": A PHONETIC FANTASY

## W.T. Goodge

The baker-man was kneading dough
And whistling softly, sweet and lough.
Yet ever and anon he'd cough
As though his head were coming ough!
"My word!" said he, "but this is rough:
This flour is simply awful stough!"

# THE DYING OF THE LIGHT

Essentially, the great heroic period of Australian traditional verse-making ended with the First World War. Henry Lawson only lived another four years and, while they continued to write, the best poetry of The Banjo and Den and many of their contemporaries was behind them.

The finest verse of this last period reeks with the regrets of old men who still remember the 'sunlit plain extended' and are now contending with the realities of old age, bustling city life, the rise of the New Woman and aching nostalgia for their youth.

In truth, while C.J. Dennis, in his famous letter to Ginger Mick, then stationed in the Middle East, painted an evocative picture of the land awaiting the return of their fighting men, the Old Australia had now disappeared. Modern Australia had begun to emerge.

# TWO MEN AND A MAID

### W.T. Goodge

Two little dudes from the George-street block,
  Up for a brief vacation!
One little girl in a neat print frock,
  Maid of the Mulga Station!
Two little dudes with walking-sticks,
Two little heads that the collars fix!
Two little hats at nine-and-six,
  Two little dudes on a station.

One little maid with a bashful smile,
  Given for a salutation;
Two little dudes of the nan-nan style,
  Bent on a captivation.
One little maid with a smile so true,
Curly hair of a nut-brown hue;
Eyes of a liquid violet blue,
  One little maid on a station.

"Didn't she fear her walks to take
  Over the grassy clearing?"
"Didn't she fear some nasty snake
  His ugly head a-rearing?"
"Sirs," she said, with an arching brow,
And a smile that was hardly a smile somehow,

"There are so many jackasses 'round here now,
  That the snakes are disappearing!"

---

A contemporary readership would have recognised that this poem echoed *Three Little Maids From School*, the opening song from Gilbert and Sullivan's acclaimed *The Mikado*, which had opened at London's Savoy Theatre in 1885.

# THE BLOCK

### C.J. Dennis

As I went strolling down The Block,
Mid marocain and crepe de chine,
My eye lit on a lovely frock –
A most enchanting shade of green.
A bouffant skirt (they're all the rage),
A deep lace yoke caught at one side,
With plain reverse of deepest sage
Had beige boleros, loosely tied.

Tight-fitting sleeves, piped with cerise,
Were appliqued with motifs rare;
A tulle scarf, falling to the knees,
Turned back and left one shoulder bare . . .
They say a most delicious maid
Inhabited this dream of bliss.
But I'd not time, I am afraid,
To notice this.

# SEA FEAR

*Charles Souter*

I can't go down to the sea again
For I am old and ailing;
My ears are deaf to the mermaid's call,
And my stiff limbs are failing.
The white sails and the tall masts
Are no longer to be seen
On the dainty clipper ships that sailed
For Hull, and Aberdeen!

I can't go down to the sea again:
My eyes are weak and bleared,
And they search again for the gallant poop
Where once I stood and steered.
There's nought but wire and boiler-plate
To meet my wand'ring gaze.
Never a sign of the graceful spars
Of the good old sailing days!

So I will sit in the little room
That all old sailors know,
And smoke, and sing, and yarn about
The ships of long ago,
'The Flying Cloud', 'The Cutty Sark',
'The Hotspur' and 'The Dart' . . .

But I won't go down to the sea again,
For fear it breaks my heart!

---

John Masefield's great marine poem, 'Sea-Fever', had been published in 1902 and become almost instantaneously famous around the English-speaking world.

# FROM THE 'BULLETIN' STAIRS

### E.J. Brady

The Mecca of Bohemian men
Was Archibald's untidy den.
Firm-footed near the portals there
Uprose, as now, a spacious stair
That carried nearer to the sky
Their inky hopes in days forebye.

This ladder to Parnassus, they
Expectant climbed – as still one may.
Oft-times upon its steps appeared
The wiry brush of Daley's beard,
Or Henry Lawson's drooped moustache
Would upward glide and downward dash.

Betimes – a gem his pocket in –
Meandered upward Roderic Quinn,
Or Bayldon bore a sonnet new,
Or Broomfield occupied the view
Insistent, in a manner vain,
On making passes with his cane.

These might encounter on the way
The "Banjo" glum, or Hugh McCrae
Or Souter with a leering cat

Or Bedford in a Queensland hat;
And other penmen debonair
Familiar with that famous stair.

The Red Tressed Maiden, all aglow,
And Clancy of the Overflow
And Dad and Dave, in company
With Ginger Mick and Jock MacFee,
From time to time, in singles, pairs,
By hand or post went up those stairs!

In his heyday, that great patron of Australian letters,
J.F. Archibald, dispensed his favours upon mendicant contributors
from his famously disordered eyrie. Among those identified
here are, *inter alia*, the poets Roderic Quinn, Arthur Bayldon
and Fred Bloomfield. According to Pat Rolfe's lively account
of *The Bulletin's* history: 'Everything accepted was paid for,
in gold at first, then by cheque with a drawing of Micawber
by Hop and the legend, "Thank Goodness, that's paid".'

# FROM THE MOODS OF GINGER MICK

### C.J. Dennis

## X. A LETTER TO THE FRONT

I 'ave written Mick a letter in reply to one uv 'is,
Where 'e arsts 'ow things is goin' where the gums an' wattles is –
So I tries to buck 'im up a bit; to go fer Abdul's fez;
An' I ain't no nob at litrachure; but this is wot I sez:

I suppose you fellers dream, Mick, in between the scraps out them
Uv the land yeh left be'ind yeh when yeh sailed to do yer share:
Uv Collins Street, or Rundle Street, or Pitt, or George, or Hay,
Uv the land beyond the Murray or along the Castlereagh.
An' I guess yeh dream of old days an' the things yeh used to do,
An' yeh wonder 'ow 'twill strike yeh when yeh've seen this business thro';
An' yeh try to count yer chances when yeh've finished wiv the Turk
An' swap the gaudy war game fer a spell o' plain, drab work.

Well, Mick, yeh know jist 'ow it is these early days o' Spring,
When the gildin' o' the wattle chucks a glow on everything.
Them olden days, the golden days that you remember well,
In spite o' war an' worry, Mick, are wiv us fer a spell.
Fer the green is on the paddicks, an' the sap is in the trees,
An' the bush birds in the gullies sing the ole, sweet melerdies;

An' we're 'opin', as we 'ear 'em, that, when next the Springtime comes,
You'll be wiv us 'ere to listen to that bird tork in the gums.

It's much the same ole Springtime, Mick, yeh reckerlect uv yore;
Boronier an' dafferdils and wattle blooms once more
Sling sweetness over city streets, an' seem to put to shame
The rotten greed an' butchery that got you on this game –
The same ole sweet September days, an' much the same ole place;
Yet, there's a sort o' *somethin'*, Mick, upon each passin' face,
A sort o' look that's got me beat; a look that you put there,
The day yeh lobbed upon the beach an' charged at Sari Bair.

It isn't that we're boastin', lad; we've done wiv most o' that –
The froth, the cheers, the flappin' flags, the giddy wavin' 'at.
Sich things is childish memories; we blush to 'ave 'em told,
Fer we 'ave seen our wounded, Mick, an' it 'as made us old.
We ain't growed soggy wiv regret, we ain't swelled out wiv pride;
But we 'ave seen it's up to us to lay our toys aside.
An' it wus you that taught us, Mick, we've growed too old fer play,
An' everlastin' picter shows, an' going' down the Bay.

An', as grown man dreams at times uv boy'ood days gone by,
So, when we're feelin' crook, I s'pose, we'll sometimes sit an' sigh.
But as a clean lad takes the ring wiv mind an' 'eart serene,
So I am 'opin' we will fight to make our man'ood clean.
When orl the stoushin's over, Mick, there's 'eaps o' work to do:
An' in the peaceful scraps to come we'll still be needin' you.
We will be needin' you the more fer wot yeh've seen an' done;
Fer you were born a Builder, lad, an' we 'ave jist begun.

There's bin a lot o' tork, ole mate, uv wot we owe to you,
An' wot yeh've braved an' done fer us, an' wot we mean to do.
We've 'ailed you boys as 'eroes, Mick, an' torked uv just reward
When you 'ave done the job yer at an' slung aside the sword.
I guess it makes yeh think a bit, an' weigh this gaudy praise;
Fer even 'eroes 'ave to eat, an' – there is other days:
The days to come when we don't need no bonzer boys to fight:
When the flamin' picnic's over an' the Leeuwin looms in sight.

Then there's another fight to fight, an' you will find it tough
To sling the Kharki clobber fer the plain civilian stuff.
When orl the cheerin' dies away, an' 'ero-worship flops,
Yeh'll 'ave to face the ole tame life – 'ard yakker or 'ard cops.
But, lad, yer land is wantin' yeh, an' wantin' each strong son
To fight the fight that never knows the firin' uv a gun:
The steady fight, when orl you boys will show wot you are worth,
An' punch a cow on Yarra Flats or drive a quill in Perth.

The gilt is on the wattle, Mick, young leaves is on the trees,
An' the bush birds in the gullies swap the ole sweet melerdies;
There's a good, green land awaitin' you when you come 'ome again
To swing a pick at Ballarat or ride Yarrowie Plain.
The streets is gay wiv dafferdils – but, haggard in the sun,
A wounded soljer passes; an' we know ole days is done;
Fer somew'ere down inside us, lad, is somethin' you put there
The day yeh swung a dirty left, fer us, at Sari Bair.

. . . over

As Den's publishers explained on the dustjacket, 'Ginger Mick was a likeable rogue who, before he answered the call to arms to defend democracy, sold fresh rabbits in the streets of Melbourne. This book tells of his tender love for Rose and his experiences at war in North Africa. The verse is full of humour and pathos and truly captures the spirit of the era.' One of Mick's worthiest contributions to the national effort was his participation in the doomed assault on Sari Bair, which proved to be the last attempt by Allied forces to regain the Gallipoli peninsula before they ultimately retreated.

*the Leeuwin looms in sight* = on the most south-westerly tip of Australia, where the Indian and Southern Oceans meet, stands Cape Leeuwin Lighthouse as a solitary sentinel.

# LIFE'S A CIGAR

### George Gordon McCrae

'Life's a cigar': the wasting body glows;
The head turns white as Kosciusko's snows;
And, with the last soul-fragrance still in air,
The ashes slowly sink in soft repose.

George Gordon McCrae (1833–1927) is sometimes referred
to as the Father of Victorian Poetry. His son, Hugh McCrae,
was prominent among the next generation of poets.

# DUSK

**C.J. Dennis**

Now is the healing, quiet hour that fills
  This gay, green world with peace and grateful rest.
Where lately over opalescent hills
  The blood of slain Day reddened all the west,
  Now comes at Night's behest,
A glow that over all the forest spills,
As with the gold of promised daffodils.
  Of all hours this is best.

It is time for thoughts of holy things,
  Of half-forgotten friends and one's own folk.
O'er all, the garden-scented sweetness clings
  To mingle with the wood fire's drifting smoke.
  A bull-frog's startled croak
Sounds from the gully where the last bird sings
His laggard vesper hymn, with folded wings;
  And night spreads forth her cloak.

Keeping their vigil where the great range yearns,
  Like rigid sentries stand the wise old gums.
On blundering wings a night-moth wheels and turns
  And lumbers on, mingling its drowsy hums
  With that far roll of drums,

Where the swift creek goes tumbling amidst the ferns . . .
Now, as the first star in the zenith burns,
   The dear, soft darkness comes.

# GLOSSARY

*banker, to run a* = when a waterway is full of water to the top of its banks

*bend* = for early Australians, a bend was usually a river bend

*billabong* = part of an old, abandoned channel of a river, which occasionally fills with water after rain

*billy* = a can in which water could be boiled and food cooked, usually two to three pints (one to two litres)

*bluey* = a swag, usually containing a blue blanket

*board* = the floor of a shearing shed

*boundary rider* = the horseman with the job of checking out a property's boundary

*chute* = when a sheep has been shorn, it is shoved unceremoniously into the chute, to slide back to the holding pen outside

*coolibah* (also 'coolabah') = a eucalypt typically found where there is occasional flooding *cornstalk* = a native-born Australian

*cove* = began its life in Australia meaning a station manager or owner

*donah* = any young woman, but particularly a sweetheart

*joe* = ewe; bare-bellied, or blue-bellied, joes are ewes with little wool on their belly

*johnny cake* = a kind of small damper

*jumbuck* = sheep, particularly a large and difficult-to-shear sheep. This term was not usually applied to a tame sheep, and it implied that the sheep was not 'owned' by the squatter or regularly shorn

*lamb down* = to spend money lavishly in the pub, usually encouraged by mine host

*mallee* = a stunted, tough eucalypt

*new-chums* = new arrivals

*nobbler* = a measure of spirits

*outback* = the sparsely populated back country

*overlander* = a drover who took stock over long distances, particularly in the far outback *peewee* = the magpie lark

*push* = C.J. Dennis defined it as 'a company of rowdy fellows gathered together for ungentle purposes'

*ringer* = fastest shearer in the shed

*rouseabouts* = unskilled workers assisting the skilled

*selector* = these were farmers who took up land leases under 'free selection' and ran small landholdings with intensive crop production – notoriously, this was hard-scrabble farming

*shanty* = a rough, and usually unlicensed, bush pub

*shaver* = a bloke wot shaves

*snagger* = an unskilful shearer who leaves 'snags' of wool on the sheep

*squatter* = originally, the squatters settled on Crown land without permission to run their stock but, over time, this was formalised and they were granted leases. Because of the size of their holdings, the word 'squatter' became synonymous with the larger and richest landowners

*sundowner* = the legendary swaggie who contrives to arrive at a farm at sundown, too late to offer his services but in time to expect the hospitality of shelter

*troopers* = police

*tucker bag* = a bag for carrying food

*waltzing Matilda* = carrying the swag

# INDEXES

## Authors

# First Lines

# Poem Titles